STOLEN INNOCENCE
Based On A True Story

White Station
PUBLISHING, LLC

A White Station Publishing, LLC Production

Text © 2023 by RONAROSE TRAIN

Copyright © 2023

All rights reserved. No part of this book may be reproduced in any form, by any electronic or mechanical means, including information storage and retrieval systems, without permission in writing from the publisher, except by a reviewer who may quote brief passages in a review.

Requests for permission to make copies of any part of this work should be sent to address below:

White Station Publishing, LLC
www.whitestationpublishing.com
First Edition
Book layout and cover design by Ira S. Van Scoyoc

Printed in the United States of America

DEDICATION

I called her Abigail.

My friend trusted me to tell her story, and we both achieved unexpected results. I believe she found peace, and I found a mission. Thanks to my Abigail for choosing me.

PREFACE

Most of my life, I lived a lie. I still do.

Now I know that I didn't have to endure evil. I wish I had had the courage to tell somebody, to believe that it's not my fault, to trust. My secrets are dark and deep, carefully hidden.

This is my story.

INNOCENCE | 1

I can't remember when Billy was not with me. He is one year younger, always my playmate and companion. He just naturally was my responsibility because no one else in our family was near our age. I believed that Billy needed protection, and it was up to me as his big sister to take care of him and teach him what to do. That's the way I've always seen our relationship. To this day, Billy is my job.

I think about him a lot while I'm on my daily runs. That's my private time, the time the memories come flooding back. My earliest recollections are warm and comforting. Those are the good ones, proof that I didn't deserve the evil that changed me.

I was a little girl in Roswell, Illinois, living in the big house with Papaw and Daisy and my brother Billy. Brent and Joyce lived there, too. I saw that my church friends had siblings, so I thought Brent and Joyce were our older brother and sister. No one explained their relationship to Billy and me, but somehow, I knew that we were family.

Billy and I were Paxtons while everyone else in the big house were Carters. I was too young to ask why our names were different, and no one bothered to talk about that, either.

Because they looked much older than our friends' parents, I wasn't sure if Daisy and Papaw were our grandparents or our mom and dad, but they were the ones who took care of us. I felt safe with them... before the evil.

I remember myself as a toddler, on the den sofa with Daisy's arm around me while she and Papaw watched television. I snuggled against her bosom, and she toyed with my thick blonde curls. I knew she loved me. She didn't have to say it, but she often did. As soon as he was tall enough to reach the cushions, Billy climbed up and burrowed into Daisy's other side. We were happy then.

Papaw was very quiet. He loved to sit in his recliner and concentrate on the TV. As young as we were, Billy and I knew he did not want to be disturbed. He generally ignored us unless he was the one taking care of us. Papaw never hugged or said he loved us. He didn't play games or read to Billy and me like Daisy did, and he never played with our curls.

Brent was a serious young man who attended the community college and spent most of his time studying. When only Brent was home to watch us, he gave us crayons and paper and we sat on the floor and drew. If we behaved so he could study, he would give us candy.

Joyce didn't have time for Billy and me. When she was home, she stayed busy doing homework and talking on the phone. Billy and I knew not to bother her.

Devout Christians like most people in our Illinois

town, our family attended a nearby church every Sunday. Billy and I learned all we needed to do to get to Heaven. I consciously tried to behave, so Jesus and Daisy would be proud of me.

My early years were a time of safety and love. I wish those were the memories that frequently return, instead of the evil.

Every morning Daisy left early to teach high school. Brent and Joyce rushed out to their schools. Papaw usually stayed with us, but he woke up grumpy. He expected Billy and me to get ready for the day by ourselves, so we dressed in the clothes Daisy had laid out the previous night. She made breakfast before she left and wrapped it to keep warm. I served Billy and me, and we ate quietly, until Papaw finished his first cup of coffee. He wasn't as irritable after that, but we still kept out of his way. If the weather was nice, Billy and I played in the yard. Our days were predictable and happy.

When I was about three and a half, a strange woman showed up and stayed with us. Daisy told us her name was Barbara. She was beautiful. I thought she looked a little like Joyce, with the same turned-up nose and bright blue eyes, but their hair was different. Joyce's was long and wavy, brown like Brent's. Barbara's cascading blonde curls looked a lot like Billy's and mine. To control her own thick curly locks, Daisy pinned her long hair on top of her head like a crown. Papaw was almost bald, and impatient with his women fixing their coiffures before church. I loved my hair, until Barbara changed my life.

Daisy wouldn't let her smoke in the house, but everyone could smell cigarette stink after Barbara came inside. As a rule, she didn't bother with Billy and me, and we instinctively kept out of her way. I observed that every night she'd dress up and various men would come to take her out. She was always happy to see them, laughing and waving as she ran to their cars. I never heard her come home but thought it must have been very late because she slept until lunch time.

Then she left us, and before I knew it, she returned. She did that again and again. Sometimes a man drove her to our house and dropped her off at the street; to me it looked like a different man each time. Barbara's frequent appearance and departure were confusing to Billy and me, and we didn't understand who she was or why she was sometimes with us. Though only a child, I noticed that our family was not the same when Barbara was present. Nobody seemed to laugh and have fun when she was there.

One visit, she brought a baby with her. At first, Billy and I were intrigued. We had no experience with babies and wanted to play with him as if he were a doll, or just watch him gurgle and flail his arms. Daisy shooed us away when we tried to touch him, but we stole peeks when she wasn't looking. He cried a lot and always seemed to need her attention. Billy and I were jealous and wished he weren't there. Daisy said he was our brother. His name was Victor, but we could call him Tory.

Sometimes Barbara disappeared and left baby Tory with us, and then Daisy didn't have any time for Billy and me. We were confused and didn't know why our world had been interrupted. We didn't like it at all.

I believed it was up to me to protect Billy and help him understand things, but I didn't understand, either.

Once as Daisy tucked me into bed, I asked, "Who was that man?"

"What man?"

"The man who brought Barbara here."

She kissed me and shook her head. "He's Tory's daddy." At my confused expression, Daisy explained. "He's Victor. Tory is named after him. Victor Sidell, Junior."

I wondered about that. Billy was William Paxton, Junior, but we didn't know what that meant. We knew nothing about a daddy. "Is Papaw our daddy?"

"No, Abby, he's your grandfather." Daisy must have realized my surprise and hugged me. Patting my cheek, she said. "Don't you think about daddies, Abby. Papaw and I will always take care of you." I did know that Daisy and even Papaw loved me and Billy. I was an innocent child, before the evil.

After a man came for Barbara and she left us again, Billy interrupted the pretend tea party I was hosting for my dolls. He looked up from steering his toy truck around our bedroom and asked me a question I had already contemplated. "Why doesn't Tory live with us all the time?"

I stopped pouring imaginary tea. "I don't know."

"Isn't he our brother?"

"Daisy says he is, and we have to love him." I was

bewildered, too. "But why doesn't he go away with Barbara?"

Billy shook his blonde curls and frowned. "I hate it when Tory stays here."

I did, too. The mystery of Tory and Barbara puzzled us both. I forgot about pouring tea as we discussed the disruptions to our childhood peace. Who was that woman, and where did she go when she left? Why did she take Tory with her only sometimes? "She scares me," I said. Billy silently shook his head and cradled his truck against his chest.

"Me, too."

I sensed something disturbing about her. "I'm glad we live with Daisy and Papaw," I said to Billy. "We're safe here." I believed that.

I was about four years old when Barbara visited so long that she moved to an apartment nearby. Tory stayed in the big house with us. He was still too little to play much, but he was our brother, and we tried to love him.

One Saturday morning, Daisy told me to dress in my Sunday clothes. "You're going to spend the day with your mother," she said.

I saw that Daisy was wearing her usual Saturday house-cleaning garments. "Why aren't you getting dressed up, too?"

She laughed. "I'm not your mother, dear," she said as

she brushed my profuse curly blonde hair. "I thought you knew."

Tearfully, I protested the shocking information. "But I want you to be my mother."

"I'm your grandmother, Abigail. That's almost as good." She took my hand as we walked, and added, "You're going with Barbara."

I shook my head in confusion, trying to make sense of that news. I was too young to have grasped the significance of last names. Now I wondered about Barbara's. Was she Paxton? Carter? Something else? I had never inquired, and no one volunteered any explanations. But weren't we one family? I had to ask an important question. "Is Billy my brother?"

"Of course he is, Abby," Daisy said.

I sighed with relief that at least something I believed was true. But I wanted to know more. "What about Joyce and Brent?"

"They're your aunt and uncle."

Why weren't they my brother and sister? I did not understand my family at all. I planned to explain this to Billy when I figured it out myself. Then a more important question required an answer. I stopped our walk and pulled Daisy's hand. She stooped to look me in the face.

"What's wrong, Abby?"

"If you're my grandmother," I asked, "why do I call you

Daisy?"

She drew me close. "You can call me anything you like," she said. "All you need to know is that I love you and will always take care of you."

I ruminated as we continued to the living room. Would I now call her Grandma? Nana? And what about Barbara? She was nothing like my friends' mothers. She was exceptionally beautiful. With her long curly blonde hair and slim figure, she looked like the television stars we watched on Sunday nights. I didn't know why she frightened me.

There was no time to process the revelations. I clung to my grandmother's hand as she brought me to Barbara. I tried to hide behind Daisy, but she knelt and kissed me goodbye.

Barbara reached for my hand and led me to her car. I reluctantly waved at my grandmother from the front seat as we drove away.

Barbara took me to an apartment complex. We walked through a courtyard of drooping plants and weathered wooden furniture, then climbed several flights of stairs to her front door. As I followed her into the small living room, the cigarette aroma told me she no longer had to smoke outdoors. She turned on the living room television, then looked to me. "We need to take a nap."

Daisy never made me nap before lunch. "Can I watch cartoons?" I asked. "I'm not sleepy."

Barbara bent to glare into my eyes. "Well, you're going to nap anyway." With her hand on my shoulder, she steered me to the bedroom. I watched her fold back the spread and lie down. "Hurry up, Abigail," she said. "I'm waiting." Then she motioned that I should lie next to her.

I hesitated. "My dress," I said, afraid that it would wrinkle.

She sighed impatiently and patted the space beside her. "You heard me."

I did what she directed, though her broad smile alarmed me. When Daisy tucked me in for a nap, it was with a quick peck on the forehead. She had never lain on my bed to sleep with me.

My mother turned to her side and visually inspected me from curly head to black patent shoes. After scrutinizing her child, Barbara lingered, stretching her arms like she was waking up, then ran her fingers through my hair. I stiffened, afraid to speak, unsure whether to run from her or lie still.

She began to touch me, tracing my eyes and mouth with her finger. "That tickles," I said as I squirmed.

"Just relax," she murmured. "You'll like this if you relax."

Increasingly apprehensive, I inched away from her as she smoothed my dress and murmured, "Pretty. So pretty." Now I expected her to tell me to take it off. I was afraid it would wrinkle, and Daisy would have to iron it. Instead, Barbara repeated, "My baby is so pretty, so very pretty."

Apprehensive and confused, I could not comprehend what was happening. I lay quietly, unsure what to do or expect. I sensed Barbara's breathing quicken, and she abruptly sat up. The sudden movement startled me.

"It's too warm," she said.

It did not seem warm to me. "I'm okay," I murmured, trying not to sound frightened.

She didn't answer. I watched her stand and take off her long flowing dress and lacy underwear. When she opened the closet door and hung her clothes, I saw shirts that looked like Papaw's. A lot of them. I wondered if one of the men lived there but was afraid to ask. She closed the door and turned to me.

"You're my little girl, Abigail," she said as she stretched her naked body next to mine.

I tried to sit up, to move away from this woman. Surely mothers were not supposed to be naked and lie with their daughters. But there was no escape. She grabbed my arm and forced me to remain in place. Turning on her side, she looked into my eyes and released her painful grip. She firmly took my hand in hers. Her voice became harsh. "You need to be a good little girl, Abigail."

I always tried to be good, but no one had ever done this to me. Daisy was loving and nurturing. She didn't frighten me. I knew that whatever was about to happen would be bad.

My mother guided my hand to her, to her breasts, to her pubic area . . . places I knew should not be touched.

"No," I sobbed, "Please no; please stop." I knew Jesus wouldn't want me to do that, but I couldn't escape. She forced me to continue touching her.

"It's okay," she soothed. "It's okay."

I didn't know why or how, but even at four, I was certain it wasn't right. "Please take me home," I begged.

"You and Billy have my hair," she murmured as she stroked my curls with her free hand. "Such thick hair." My tears and pleas had no effect as she continued guiding me. "So pretty," she moaned and writhed, firmly using my hand to stroke herself.

My mother finally ceased moving.

Again, she abruptly sat up. "It's time for you to sleep now."

She left me in the bed while she spent time in the adjoining bathroom. I heard her humming a lively tune as she returned to the closet to don her dress. Without another word to me, she left the bedroom, closing the door behind her.

Afraid, I cried quietly while listening to Barbara running water in the kitchen, opening and closing the refrigerator door, and moving around the apartment. When I heard her turning the bedroom door handle, I closed my eyes.

Her voice sounded friendly, as if we had spent a lovely day together. As if she had not introduced me to her evil. "Wake up, Abigail. It's time to go home."

Frightened, unsure what she would do next, I followed her into the living room and sat in the chair she indicated. She leaned forward, and face to face, she glared into my eyes. "You are a bad little girl, Abigail."

Confused, I didn't know what I had done that was bad. I knew I shouldn't have touched her in those places. Even though she made me do it, I accepted that it must have been my fault.

"This is our secret," she said. "You can never tell anyone." She paused and shook her head. "If you ever tell anyone, anyone at all, they will send you away."

That day changed my life.

HAPPY DAYS | 2

I believed Barbara. If I told my grandmother what I had done, surely Daisy would punish me. She would send me away.

Smiling expectantly, Daisy opened the car door for me. "Did you two have a good time?"

The Bible said to never tell a lie, but Barbara's frown warned me to give the right answer. What could I do? Fear forced me to lie. No matter what I responded, I was a bad girl.

"Yes," I said, "we had fun."

Shortly after that evil day, my mother left as mysteriously as she had appeared, taking Tory with her. Her departure did not erase the memory or the secret. Guilt and fear became my life-long companions.

Billy and I shared an upstairs room next to Daisy and Papaw, each of us in a twin bed. Nightmares filled my sleep, punctuated by shrieks that awakened my brother and brought Daisy running to me. She held me as I sobbed, stroking my hair. "It's going to be okay. It's going to be okay." They were the same words and actions her daughter had repeated as she guided my hand.

With time, I suffered only occasional nightmares, but Barbara had changed everything for me. No amount of washing could cleanse the memory of her fondling my curls while guiding my hand. I always felt dirty when I fixed my hair. With that constant reminder, I made sure to be a good girl and do everything expected of me and more.

Each night before bed, I prayed that no one would send me away.

Every Sunday, Daisy woke Billy and me early and we dressed in our best clothes. In church we learned all about Jesus and his love for us. I was afraid He knew what I had done, so I prayed harder in services and sang louder than the other children in the choir so he would forgive my sins.

After services, my grandparents loaded us in the car, and we'd drive to our favorite Roswell restaurant for their Sunday buffet. Brent usually stayed longer at church, but Joyce was excited to go with us. Billy and I enjoyed her rare attention. Every morsel of Sunday time with the teenager made me miss her more when she returned to her normal behavior and couldn't be bothered with us youngsters.

"Let me guess," Papaw would tease me. "You're getting the Salisbury steak and mashed potatoes."

We laughed because that's what I always ate, mainly because that's what Daisy inevitably chose. Papaw's repeated joke was a welcome change from his usual serious behavior, making Sundays even more special to me. Though that buffet occupied my thoughts every day as I considered what I would eat the following Sunday, I couldn't resist mimicking Daisy's choices. I would do anything to please my grandmother. When she said, "Go choose our desserts, Abby," I swelled with pride. Daisy was the most important person in my life. If she were happy with me, maybe she would never send me away.

On those Sundays, I took my after-lunch nap with a joyous heart. For another week, I was safe.

Billy and I were full of energy after our rest but played quietly until Papaw and Daisy opened their door and came looking for us. Daisy worked hard all week and needed a respite. I tried to keep my brother interested in a puzzle or game so they could sleep as long as they wanted. I knew Papaw didn't mean to be grumpy, and he always made sure someone took care of us. I thought he deserved to nap, too. The sight of their rested, smiling faces made me happy, and I couldn't wait for our special Sunday evenings.

Billy and I sat on the floor with Joyce, ready for the television shows to begin. Brent and Daisy settled on the sofa, and Papaw claimed his big chair. We gobbled bottomless bowls of popcorn and watched Lawrence Welk, Ed Sullivan, Red Skelton, and Route 66. Then Daisy put my brother and me in the bath and laid out our outfits to be ready for the next day. She shopped at the best department store in Roswell and bought us the nicest clothes and shoes. My grandmother made sure we were dressed well.

Daisy herself was immaculate. She went to teach school

every day dressed in a suit and matching shoes. She smelled of Tabu. The scent lingered hours after she left the house. To this day I keep a bottle of that fifties perfume just to remind me of my grandmother. She was exquisite, with fine features and a stately bearing. Her dramatic hairdo was always just so, with a wave in the front and a tight braid that she laid behind it. Nobody could tell that she had beautiful long hair, but everyone complimented the unique style. To me, Daisy's inner beauty surpassed her physical attractiveness. Her sincere smile, her gentleness, her kindness to Billy and me, and her soft-spoken voice conveyed her love. My grandmother was the most important influence in my life, and I wanted to be just like her.

But that was impossible. I was a bad person.

MAMA FAYE | 3

I can't remember when Mama Faye came to live in the little house next door to our big one because she was always there. We knew she was Daisy's mother, with the same gentle soul as her daughter. She lived alone but was always cheerful. Billy and I thought she was very old because of her gray hair and sagging chin that wobbled when she laughed. Mama Faye was a constant hugger. We felt loved as we nestled against her bosom while she read to us.

Mama Faye wasn't stand-offish like Papaw's mother. Tall and lean and gruff like her son, Nana Carter did not seem interested in us little kids. Daisy told us we should be nice to her because it was hard to travel from Alabama to visit us in Illinois. We did not see Nana very often and didn't enjoy it when we did. Billy and I stayed out of her way.

Occasionally we went to the stores with Papaw or played with our toys while he watched television or worked at the dining room table. But he was only an interim babysitter, keeping an eye on us until someone else could take over. Most days he took us to Mama Faye and went to his office.

We loved to be with Daisy's mother. "Hurry up, Billy," I

would yell as we raced across the yard to Mama Faye in the little house. "I smell something good."

"Cookies," my brother laughed as he tagged behind me, repeatedly pushing his blonde curls away from his eyes. Mama Faye always had something delicious waiting for us.

A year faster and taller than Billy, I breathlessly got to her door first.

"Come on in." She greeted us with a smile and hugs before leading us to the living room.

"What are we going to do today?" I anticipated the fun our great grandmother had in store for us. Some days she read stories or taught us to play dominoes.

"We're going to eat cookies," she smiled mischievously, pointing to the plate of homemade treats. "Take one and put it on the table," she directed.

Billy and I looked longingly at them, teased by the tantalizing aroma of warm chocolate chips.

"If I tell you to take another, what number would that be?"

"Two!" we said.

"And what's next?"

"Three!" After counting out the tempting cookies, we subtracted one at a time, aiming for our mouths. That was the best part of the lesson.

Mama Faye was a widow long before I was born. We never knew Daddy Will, but she told us about him.

"Wilbur left me with property and money in the bank. Daisy doesn't have to worry about me." Billy and I didn't know what that meant, but we were sure glad that our grandmother didn't need to worry.

"Your great grandaddy was a smart man," she said. "He was an entrepreneur."

We learned the meaning of that big word and marveled at all the ways he knew to make money. Before we even went to kindergarten, Billy and I dreamed of being entrepreneurs when we grew up. We played "store" and "office" and argued about which one of us got to be the boss. We didn't know then that while Mama Faye fed and played with us, she was teaching us to count, write, and solve math problems. When we started public school, we already knew so much because of her.

Billy and I loved to play outdoors in our yard. Mama Faye could watch over us from her back window or sitting on the bench Papaw had built. When we were about three and four years old, for some reason, my brother and I believed there was gold hidden on our property. With our little metal shovels, we dug holes in search of buried treasure. We penetrated the dirt so deeply in one spot that we hit a wet area. Water gushed unchecked.

Billy jumped up and danced in delight, his curls bouncing. "Gold!"

I joined him, sure we had found pirate's booty. Instead, we must have pierced a rusting water line. Mama Faye rushed out of her house, frantically calling "Are you alright?" She checked us for cuts and bruises as we danced out of her grasp, then she ran into the big house to get Papaw. Luckily, he was working at home that day and cut off the water flooding his property. Of course, he fussed at us, but he left the discipline to Mama Faye. She sat us down on her sofa and talked to us about right and wrong. We didn't know what was wrong about digging in dirt, but we nodded respectfully. After that, she found other entertainment for us.

Mama Faye must have been in her seventies then. One day I realized she wasn't there. She was always home. We did not understand why she went somewhere else. Time was meaningless to me at such an early age. I didn't know how long our great grandmother had been missing until one day Daisy didn't leave to teach school.

"Get dressed," she told us. "We're going to Saint Louis."

Billy and I got in the car with our grandparents, excited to see the big city we had only heard about.

"Sit in the front between Papaw and me," Daisy told Billy, while I squeezed in the back with Brent and Joyce. I noticed my grandmother wiping her eyes and blowing her nose. There was a sadness in the atmosphere. Nobody talked much. Billy was too far from me to play rock, paper, scissors, so I watched out the window and counted the red cars we passed and fell asleep until I felt the car maneuvering.

Papaw parked in front of a big building with signs I couldn't read, but the people in wheelchairs and the ambulances screaming up the driveway told me it was a hospital. I didn't know why we were there. Scared and confused, Billy and I held hands as our family found our way to the correct room.

"Mama Faye!" Billy yelled, running to her bed. He was so happy to see her that he tried to climb up to her, but was too little. Daisy picked him up and he snuggled beside our great grandmother, his head on her shoulder.

With a beautiful smile, she weakly hugged Billy to her. "I love you so much," she whispered as she feebly stroked his curls. I could barely hear her. I wanted to ask Daisy what was wrong with her, but my grandmother was not paying attention to anyone but her mother.

Everyone cried and told Mama Faye we loved her, too. She passed away with her arm around my brother, quietly and peacefully leaving us to join her Wilbur.

Daisy saw and began screaming for the nurses. Papaw took Billy and me out into the hall to find a waiting area. Joyce and Brent stayed with us so Papaw could help our grandmother. We stayed there a long time, crying and trying to understand what had happened to Mama Faye.

Back in Roswell, for a few days Billy and I were alone in the big house with a babysitter while everyone else in our family were gone. I later realized that's when they went to the funeral. Our Mama Faye rests in the cemetery with Wilbur and all her relatives in a small town where they once lived.

We loved her so much. It was the first loss we experienced in our lives. Mama Faye was a warm, wonderful, good woman. With her we had felt safe and loved. I think of her often.

PURGATORY | 4

Soon after our family returned from burying Mama Faye, a man brought Barbara and Tory back to us. Billy and I hadn't seen them in a while. I heard her talking to Daisy about Mama Faye's funeral, so I guessed she had been there. I'm sure that's why she decided to come home again. Frightened, I remembered her last visit and prayed Jesus wouldn't allow her to do bad things to me.

After dinner one evening, I was in my bedroom playing with my dolls. "Put on your prettiest dress, Abigail." I looked up at Barbara in confusion.

"Is it Sunday?"

"No, it's not, but we are going to a special place."

"Is Billy going, too?"

She shook her head. "He's only three," she said, holding out a dress for me. "He's too young to behave." She laid out my patent leather shoes and the lace-trimmed socks I wore to church. "Put on clean panties, too," she said.

Confused and frightened, I dressed as she instructed. "Where are we going?" She didn't answer. "Why do we have to go tonight?" Ignoring my questions, my mother urged me to hurry and buckle my shoes.

We went downstairs to the den, and she told my grandparents we would be home soon. They looked up from their television show.

"Be a good girl for your mother," Daisy said with a smile.

"My friends are waiting to meet you." Barbara knelt to fold the lace on my sock.

Other than in church, the adults in my family rarely socialized. I had never seen anyone else with Barbara other than the men in the cars, and none of us had visitors in our home.

"I didn't know you had friends," I said as she arranged my uncontrollable curls.

She glanced up at Daisy and then glared at me. "I have lots of them," she said, suddenly putting on a big smile and a chirpy voice. "Everyone wants to see my pretty little girl." She told me to kiss Daisy goodbye.

Barbara and I walked up the long driveway to the sidewalk. "You'll like this place. If you're a good girl, we'll buy a snack at the convenience store next door." I planned to be very good. "There's a pool out back," she said. "One day we'll go swimming, but not tonight."

I knew we couldn't swim that night because I was wearing my prettiest church dress, but I eagerly anticipated the time when we could go into the pool. "Can Billy come, too?" I asked, walking fast to keep up with my mother's brisk stride.

"Um, sure," she said, taking my hand and pulling me along. "Keep up, Abigail. We're going to be late."

Our destination was close by, and since Barbara didn't have a car, we walked the few blocks. I had seen the little building in passing but didn't know what it was.

"That must be your little girl," the man at the door said as Barbara gave him money. "The guys are over there." He pointed to people who were laughing and beckoning to Barbara.

She waved to them and took my hand again as we made our way to the group. "See, Abigail, I have lots of friends."

The men and women seemed to be having fun, ordering drinks even for me. I liked the pink juice and asked for three cherries when Barbara told me I could have another one. Her friends were nice to me, exclaiming how pretty I was, and touching my blonde curls. The music made me want to dance and sing like I saw in the Sunday night television shows, and Barbara noticed.

"My little Ginger Rogers has rhythm," she laughed, and her friends laughed, too. She lifted me up onto the bar. "Dance for us, Abigail." And I did.

The men and women talked about me while I pretended that I was on stage, a television star.

"Isn't she adorable?"

"Look at that gorgeous head of hair."

"Just the cutest thing ever."

And Barbara encouraged them while she touched my clothes, my hair, rubbed my legs. "Isn't she pretty?" Then the men began touching me. "She's pretty, isn't she?" Barbara cooed as she let them rub my leg, fondle my dress, breathe their whiskey breath in my face.

She took me off the bar and we went outdoors to the patio area. When I saw the pool, I was excited. "Are we going swimming now?" Then I realized I couldn't get my best dress wet. "Did you bring my bathing suit?"

Barbara laughed. "Isn't she smart?" she asked the men who had accompanied us. "She wants to go swimming." She leaned down and whispered in my ear. "Maybe another time. Tonight, we're having fun with my friends." Her breath smelled, too. It was very late before she walked me home. I was tired and afraid that Daisy was awake. If she asked me why my dress was wrinkled, I would have to tell her it was from lying on the lounge chair while the men rubbed me.

But Barbara frightened me. "You were a bad girl again."

"I don't want to be bad." I pleaded with my mother. "Don't make me see your friends again," I begged. "Why do they touch me like that?"

She stumbled a bit and answered with venom. "You'll see my friends any time I want," she said. "They like you." Barbara jerked my hand so hard it hurt my shoulder. Her next words confirmed my fear. "That's another secret."

I looked at her and knew what had happened wasn't right. Barbara didn't make me sing and dance at Daisy's house. My mother's friends didn't come to Daisy's house and touch me all over. But I also knew that I had to keep our secret from Daisy. I believed if my grandmother knew what I was doing, she would send me away.

Following one after-dinner visit to the bar, I gathered the courage to speak about it. "I don't want to go with Barbara anymore," I said to Daisy as she tucked me into bed. "I want to stay home."

My grandmother told me everything would be alright. "Barbara won't be here very long, and you should spend time with her while you can."

"But I want to be with you and Papaw."

"Barbara is your mother, Abby. You must honor thy mother." She kissed me. "Now go to sleep. We don't want to wake Billy."

Barbara came and went again and again. I was relieved when she was elsewhere but plunged into despair each time she returned. Whether Barbara was present or not, our secrets haunted me.

One afternoon when I was in first grade, Papaw was preoccupied as he walked us home. He was quieter than usual and didn't even glance at Billy's kindergarten project. I gave my brother a warning look. Something was bothering Papaw. If we disturbed him, he could be grumpy and fuss at us. It was my job to keep us out of trouble.

The reason for his silence was in our den. I saw Barbara sitting on the sofa, holding a bag of ice to her cheek.

My nightmares had come to life.

"Hello, Abigail. Hi, William."

Neither one of us answered our mother. We froze and stared at Barbara's bruised and swollen face.

Home early from teaching school, Daisy had been offering a cookie to entice Tory, who nestled under the coffee table. Daisy left Tory in his grotto to hustle Billy and me into the kitchen. "Don't worry about your mother," she said, pouring milk for us. Billy took a cookie from the bag, but I was too upset to eat. Daisy must have noticed my hesitation. "Barbara's been in an accident. She and Tory have come to visit."

A few days later Barbara left in a car with a man and Tory stayed with us.

He was only about three and did anything he wanted. Even when Barbara was present, she either ignored or laughed at her son's mischief, setting the pattern for his lifelong disregard for authority and accountability.

Tory's behavior got under Papaw's skin and made him even grumpier than usual. No reprimands discouraged Tory from climbing on, crawling under, or damaging our grandparents' furniture. The worst incident was the missing pocket watch. It had been Papaw's father's and it meant a lot to our grandfather. The whole family searched for it, until Tory proudly said, "It's buried treasure."

Daisy was the first to understand and knelt to speak with Tory. "Where is it buried, matey?"

He pointed. "Over there, with all the booty."

"We'll move the treasure to a safer place," my grandmother said. Her stern look told Papaw that she had it handled.

Tory led us to the big oak tree behind the house and we searched all around and in it. Papaw's keepsake wasn't there. We followed Tory all over the yard while he tried to remember where he hid it, but we never found that watch. Our grandpa was so upset that soon Barbara showed up to take Tory away.

Before long, she came back, and to my horror, moved in with us again.

"Put on this dress, Abigail," Barbara said one night after dinner. I took the dress as she laid out my ruffled socks and Sunday shoes. That could only mean we were going to see the men. "There are no clean panties in your drawer. You don't have to wear any tonight."

That didn't seem right. I never dressed without underwear. I brightened with an idea. "Are we going swimming tonight? I could wear my bathing suit." With a glimmer of hope, I said, "Billy can come with us. He likes to swim, too."

"Sure," she said. "We'll bring Billy." She nodded to me and called for him to put on his suit. I smiled in relief, but Barbara didn't tell me to change clothes. She didn't put my bathing suit in the bag with Billy's towel.

Downstairs, Barbara told my grandparents we were going to the pool with her friends. As we left, they murmured goodbye and gave me a quick kiss. I've always wondered why Daisy didn't seem to notice I was wearing church clothes to go swimming.

Billy and I held hands as we followed our mother the few blocks to the bar. Her friends were there already, the same men I had seen on many previous nights when she lived with us. There were some new faces, too. Every one of them was laughing, drinking beer, and looking at me. They offered Barbara a beer and began touching me. My hair. My dress. My legs.

Billy bounced from foot to foot and begged, "Can I go in now?" He ran to the door Barbara indicated as he yelled, "Last one in is a rotten egg." He probably wouldn't have waited for me, even if I had been allowed to join him.

"Stay in the shallow end," Barbara said as we followed him out back. "I'm going to be too busy to watch you." She laughed with the group who had followed us outside.

Billy occasionally yelled for me to stop playing with the men and join him in the pool. I don't think he realized what they were doing to me, nor understood it was wrong. Fully believing Barbara's threats of banishment, I submitted to her commands. If I had told an adult that I was being abused, would anyone believe me? Would anything be done? Would my life have changed?

Every trip to the bar filled me with the certain knowledge that men should not touch me in those places. Honoring my mother burdened me with guilt and fear. Sometimes Barbara invited Billy as a justification for us to go there, but I wore my church dresses while he had on a bathing suit. How could Daisy and Papaw ignore those signs? I never heard them express doubts.

I was old enough to know that our secrets were bad and

therefore I believed I was bad. Vowing to be a good girl for my grandmother, I lived in fear and confusion as Barbara continued to leave us and return without warning.

Though my buried secrets haunted me, I nevertheless presented to others a seemingly normal childhood. No one detected that I was being abused. I easily excelled in kindergarten and elementary school, thanks to Mama Faye's lessons.

Sometimes Billy and I got into trouble as we grew older and more adventurous, but we were just kids having fun. We loved climbing out the upstairs window onto the tree branches and jumping down to the ground. The Murdock brothers were our neighbors and partners in mischief. We built forts under the bushes or played hide and seek, delighted in making up games, and told frightening ghost stories. The four of us spent many happy hours until we reluctantly answered the summons to dinner.

I was eight years old on November 22nd, 1963, when our principal unexpectedly made an announcement on the loudspeaker. I heard him clear his throat and say, "School is dismissed early today, students. Please wait for your parents to pick you up." Since we lived in the next block, Billy and I walked to the corner as usual and saw Papaw already waiting for us. He took our hands and we went to the big house without saying a word. There were no inquiries about our lessons that day or requests to see our drawings to tape to the fridge. Billy and I looked at each other, suspecting that something bad must be happening. I worried that Daisy knew what I had done with Barbara.

Papaw sat us down on the sofa in the den across from the kitchen and we three watched the television. Joyce and Brent soon joined us, and Daisy did, too. I was old enough to understand that our President was dead. We cried and remained glued to the TV for days.

The world changed with the assassination of JFK. My own world also shifted forever. After a long absence, that night Barbara came back to Roswell and brought Tory with her. They never left.

SURPRISE | 5

My grandparents set up a bedroom downstairs for Barbara and Tory. The tension that had filled our home with every visit now permanently permeated the atmosphere. My only escape was to the pack of rambunctious brothers who lived next door. Billy and I spent carefree times with the four Murdock boys. The only girl in the gang, I happily suffered their constant teasing.

High in the tallest tree, I frequently indulged my love of singing. At the top of my voice, I pretended to be the star of an imaginary television show, undaunted by any one of the Murdocks yelling, "What do you think you are, a bird?"

"Yes, I am a beautiful bird!" In my mind I flew high into the sky, warbling my freedom from my mother and her evil. I wasn't ugly. I wasn't bad.

Billy and I tried to include Tory in our games and asked him to watch television with us, but he always found a way to torment.

"He lies," Billy complained to me after our younger brother ran to our grandmother. "He broke my model plane, and now he's saying I did it."

"He's only four," I said, gathering my homework papers Tory had scattered around the den. "Sharing is hard for him. Tory's never lived with anyone but his mother."

"But he's here with us now, Abby. Why does he think he can do anything he wants?"

"I guess Barbara lets him."

"Just keep him away from me," seven-year-old Billy pleaded. "He may be little, but he's mean."

Both of us spent most of the time in our bedroom with the door closed. Billy wanted to escape Tory, and I needed distance from Barbara. But when everyone else was out or busy, she found me.

"It's our secret time, Abigail."

At eight years of age, I was certain our covert activity was a sin, but nothing stopped Barbara from making me pleasure her. And I was horrified when she touched me, too. I cringed as she closed and locked my bedroom door.

"You're a bad girl, Abigail," she repeated as she stroked my hair and my body. Our secret was now so frightening that I feared my grandparents had to find out soon. How could they not know what was happening in their own home? "You can't tell anyone what we do. They will send you away."

I had no concept of where "away" would be, but it wouldn't be home. It wouldn't be safe. It wouldn't be with Daisy and Papaw. So I was a good little girl and kept my mouth shut. I went to school and church, watched Billy to protect him from Barbara and Tory, and prayed that Jesus knew it wasn't my fault that I was bad.

My mother and brother had been with us about five months when Billy came to me. "Where did Papaw go?"

"I don't know," I said. "I asked Daisy yesterday. She told me we would find out soon."

"Papaw never left us before."

I was sure he was finding a place to send me. What other reason could there be? "We have to wait," I said. "Don't worry, Billy." I was more frightened than ever.

He returned after ten days and delivered a grand surprise. An engineer, Papaw was meticulous and had researched to find exactly what he wanted. He had taken a train from Roswell, Illinois, to Detroit, Michigan, to buy a thirty-foot-long FMC motor coach and then drive it all the way home. The monstrous house on wheels now sat in our long driveway. We had never seen anything so big.

Billy discovered the closet-sized bathroom. "You can even flush the toilet," he exclaimed.

Tory climbed up to the top bunk and beat his chest. "Me Tarzan!"

Daisy and I explored the kitchen, and Joyce sat in the driver's seat, pretending to navigate the huge bus through mountains. Papaw sat all of us down and gave us news that was meant to be even more sensational than the surprise of the motor coach. "We're all going on a trip," he said.

"Everyone?" I asked, dreading his answer.

"Of course," he said. "You, Billy, Joyce, and Tory. You're going to see places you'll remember the rest of your lives."

Billy was practical. "Where will everybody sleep?"

Papaw uttered a rare laugh. "Anywhere we can find a space."

"We'll have to share," Daisy cautioned.

"I wish Mama Faye could come," I said with sadness for our loss.

"I do, too," my grandmother said, "but the trip would have been too hard for her."

I missed Mama Faye and sometimes dreamed of her, awaking with regret that she was gone. Then, with a bright thought, I hoped that Barbara would stay in Roswell. Before I could ask, Barbara gave me a direct look and a nod. My mother would be on board with the rest of us. My heart sank.

"We'll leave when school's out in May," Daisy said. "It will be an adventure."

Everybody but Brent would pile into the coach, and we would tour all summer. My family began planning the exciting trip. Every evening after dinner, everyone pored over magazines and books to learn about the sights we would visit. While the others studied and debated, I was filled with anxiety.

Daisy noticed my silence. "Don't you want to read these

brochures, Abby?"

"No thanks. You can decide where we're going."

"But it's so much fun to know all about the places before we get there."

"I think my stomach hurts." I wanly smiled and escaped upstairs to my bedroom.

In my dreams, I saw the close quarters I would occupy with the woman who did such vile things to me. The nightmares filled me with horror that my grandparents would discover our secret. If they sent me away, I might never return.

⑥ | OUR ADVENTURE

May 1964 finally arrived, and school closed for the summer. Our family boarded our home on wheels and headed west. We were the main attraction at every site and sight we visited. No one had ever seen anything like our FMC motor coach, and people flocked to view it. Papaw never tired of showing off that huge vehicle to the jealous men, and Daisy explained her kitchen's hidden attributes to the incredulous women. Billy and I were heady with importance as we strutted around the children who came to gape. We proudly told them about the bathroom and bunk beds.

Four-year-old Tory, who couldn't sit still, always got into mischief. He literally ran circles around everyone as we entertained our audiences. Teen-aged Joyce was charged with keeping him corralled while Barbara smoked somewhere, but taming Tory was an impossible job. My young aunt focused instead on the cute boys who were drawn to the coach like fish to bait. There was always one to reel in.

Papaw drove the bus west through several states on our route to Nevada. We kids kept busy playing board games and cards. I tried never to be alone in the coach at a stop, keeping a watchful eye for Barbara. Would she do secret things to me on our bus? Could she isolate me from everyone else for a few moments of her pleasure? I lived in fear of my mother's advances and our discovery.

Papaw timed our Las Vegas approach for nighttime arrival. We were spellbound. "Look at the lights!" everyone exclaimed. "They're brighter than the stars!"

"And there are more lights than stars," Daisy said.

"Look!" I shrieked, pointing upward at a flashing marquee. "Red Skelton!" Sure enough, our Sunday night favorite was performing there. "Can we go?" I begged.

Of course, my grandparents wouldn't spend so much money for us to see him in person. At my age, just being in the same city meant a lot to me.

"Let's watch out for him," Daisy said. "Maybe he'll walk down the street, and we can catch a glimpse."

I studied every single face we passed, but Mr. Skelton must not have been a walker. Nevertheless, the possibility of seeing him was exciting and memorable.

Papaw drove on narrow, curving roads with increasing skill. The Grand Canyon awed us, and the Redwood Forest dwarfed us. We took hundreds of photos on that trip, but no image can convey the effect of those miracles of nature. My soul soared at the sights. For those moments I felt the glory of God. I wanted Him to take care of me, to forgive me for my secrets. The canyon and the forest were proof He could do wonderful things. Maybe He would keep Daisy from sending me away. I tried even harder to help my grandparents, to be good, to be worthy.

Papaw said we couldn't afford to waste money on restaurants, so we shopped together at local groceries. It was fun to all pitch in to prepare meals. Daisy made me her sous chef in our compact kitchen. We prepared delicious full course dinners and towering sandwiches. We enjoyed eating picnic style in roadside parks and various parking lots. Despite Barbara's looming presence, our adventure was a happy time for me. Those memories bring me joy even now.

Papaw drove our coach up the California coast from stop to stop according to the itinerary developed by everyone but me, touring popular tourist sites. We rode every Disneyland ride and posed for photos with the famous characters.

So absorbed reading the famous names on the stars embedded in the sidewalk in front of Grauman's Chinese Theater, I walked into a parking meter. When I regained consciousness, I was face down on the ground. Daisy hugged me so tightly it was hard to breathe.

We hugged the Pacific coast on the 101, traveling north to San Francisco through dense urban scenery. The scenic drive to Seattle gave Joyce time to teach Billy and me gin rummy before we reached the remnant of the 1962 World's Fair.

We tilted our heads to see the 605-foot-high tip of the Space Needle. "Are we going all the way up?" Billy asked Papaw.

"As far as the Observation Deck," he said with a smile.

"But you won't have to climb stairs."

Our grandparents herded us to the line of tourists queuing for an elevator. We spent the wait keeping tabs on Tory. He explored anything he saw, wandering away with no regard for safety. Billy and I retrieved him several times while Joyce trolled for the cutest boys. Barbara found a group of friendly men and paid no attention to her vanishing son.

It was a 43-second ride but seemed much longer. Too many people had packed the elevator, producing aromas of onions and perspiration. Billy wrinkled his nose and exclaimed aloud what everyone else had to be thinking. "Phew! It stinks in here."

Many passengers laughed, but a few faces turned bright red. Daisy gave him a wink, and Papaw covered his mouth to stifle a chuckle. I just wanted to get out and breathe fresh air.

Joyce shrieked as we stepped out of the elevator. "I'm falling!"

"I'm flying!" Billy yelled.

I had the sensation of floating above the fairgrounds, suspended in air, defying gravity. The Observation Deck floor was glass, as were the walls and benches. Papaw and Daisy allowed Billy, Tory, and me to run free, pretending to fly the full circumference of the sky-high structure. We didn't realize it was more than an illusion. It was a dream.

In August we drove to Wyoming and saw Old Faithful and Yellowstone. Driving the unwieldy bus on the winding roads must have been challenging for Papaw, but we kids thought it great fun.

After our memorable adventure, we came to the end of our itinerary. Papaw stopped in Topeka, Kansas, to visit his brother, our Uncle Hank, whom I had never before met. When we left his family, Papaw drove for a few hours and pulled our coach into a park with a pond.

"Can we swim?" Billy asked our grandparents. Tory had already run to the edge and looked ready to wade in.

Daisy glanced at Papaw and nodded. "You children can take off your shoes and just put your feet in the water while Joyce, your mother, and I fix lunch."

We were only allowed to stand along the shallow edge, but Papaw didn't scold us when Billy and I followed Tory's lead and splashed a little water on ourselves. We all knew that Kansas had been the last stop. It was a lovely day for a picnic lunch, and reminiscing. We talked about our favorite sights and experiences. It was hard to name just a few. The memories were meant to be cherished forever.

I welcomed a nap as we drove away, falling asleep as I thought about soon sleeping in my own bed, and leisure time before beginning fourth grade. I was ready to go home.

WHY? | 7

It was a peaceful nap until I felt a sudden sway. Jostled to the edge of the bunk, I blinked awake. Papaw had turned the coach sharply to maneuver the huge bus into a parking lot within a complex of stately red brick buildings.

"Are we still in Kansas?" I asked as I climbed down to join Tory and Billy at the biggest side window. "Why are we here?"

No one answered my questions.

"Is this a school?" Billy asked. We had seen pictures of Uncle Brent's divinity college, and there was a resemblance.

Papaw had chosen to park opposite a massive building. The sign said Administration. I didn't remember this place listed on our itinerary.

My grandmother stood and took Tory's hand as Papaw quietly opened the door. "Billy, Abigail, I want you to come with Tory and me." Daisy exited the FMC with no further explanation.

We were confused but followed them up the sidewalk and through the heavy double doors to a lobby. "Wait here,"

Daisy told us. "I'll be right back."

We watched her walk to a window with a view into an office. She gave her name to the woman behind the sliding glass.

"Oh yes," the lady said. "Come with me."

My grandmother instructed us to sit on the chairs lining the wall. "Don't worry," she said. "It may take me a while, but I'll be back for you."

"What's happening?" Billy asked me as Tory began crawling under the chairs. "Why are we here?"

"I don't know," I said, "but I'm scared."

"Me, too."

It didn't take long for Daisy to return. "This is Mr. Johnstone," she said. "He will take care of you now."

We didn't understand.

Daisy bent down to Billy and me and put a hand on each of our shoulders. "This is where you children are going to live."

"Here?" I tried to comprehend. "Are you going to live here, too?"

Daisy looked into my eyes with tears in hers and shook her head. "No, Abby." That was all she said. I thought she was trying not to cry.

"Why?" I asked as I stood. Tears streamed down my face. "I've been good."

She didn't respond to my pleas, nor to Billy's. Daisy motioned for us to walk outside with her while Mr. Johnstone attempted to lure Tory out from under a chair.

I didn't see Papaw, Barbara, and Joyce anywhere. I couldn't see inside the motor coach because the curtains were closed, but I thought I detected a flutter. They must have been watching while hiding from our view.

"Those are ours!" Billy pointed to the line of suitcases on the sidewalk.

"We've packed your clothes," Daisy managed to say as she dropped to her knees and sobbed. She hugged us so long and cried so desperately that I couldn't understand why she would do this to us. How could our grandparents leave us here? Did they discover my secrets? What was this place?

Occasionally that scene replays in my memory, leaving me as devastated and desperate as I was in that moment so many years ago.

Daisy told me how much she loved us, and that we would be okay. She shook with sobs as she stood and kissed our foreheads. Despite our pleas, she turned and walked away from us as the door to the bus opened. I saw Papaw help her up the step. When he closed the door without acknowledging his hysterical grandchildren, my heart shattered. How could he hate me so much? The answer was clear. He had discovered my secrets.

Even Tory was whimpering as he realized he had to remain. Billy and I frantically tried to follow our grandmother to the bus, but Mr. Johnstone held us back.

To my horror, Papaw drove away. We watched everyone we loved and everything we knew exit the parking lot and our lives. From the wide back window, Joyce waved to her deserted niece and nephews. My family had given us to a stranger.

I knew it was my fault. I could understand why they didn't want me any longer, but why did my brothers have to suffer, too? My guilt was overwhelming and remained with me for many years. I was eight, Billy seven, and Tory five.

We stood on the sidewalk for a while after the coach disappeared from our sight, desperately crying and pleading for our family to return. Billy and I begged Mr. Johnstone to make them come back for us.

He spoke to us with patience and kindness, allowing our grief. "You'll be fine." His assurance meant nothing. He took Tory's hand. "Come with me, children."

Quietly crying, confused, and heartbroken, I obediently followed. We were now residents of the Stillbrook, Missouri, Christian Children's Home.

THE HOME | 8

My brothers and I had gone from a loving home and family to no home and no family. Distraught, I believed that I alone was responsible for our abandonment. Billy and Tory were so little they needed my protection. As the big sister, I vowed to be their surrogate mother and guardian. It was up to me to keep them safe.

Still sniffling, I walked with Mr. Johnstone and my brothers to a dormitory. "You boys will live here," he told them as we approached a woman who seemed to be waiting for us in the large living room. Billy had stopped crying but clung to my hand.

Mr. Johnstone bent to face the boys. "Mrs. Atkins is your house mother."

"Are you Billy or Tory?" She reached out to take Billy's hand from mine. "Let's go see your room."

I helplessly watched them leave me. Too incredulous to ask what would now happen to me, I turned to Mr. Johnstone. I surely was a portrait of fear and confusion.

"We're going to drive to your dormitory," Mr. Johnstone said to me, not unkindly. "Don't worry, Abigail, they will be fine here."

How could they be fine? They had been abandoned twice in one day. Guilt and anguish consumed me, and I sobbed in despair. I leaned against the door as Mr. Johnstone navigated his car up a long hill. Through my tears, I saw a church with a tall steeple and understood that though we were among strangers, they were Christians. Now I knew why our family gave us away. I was a sinner. My guilt was unbearable.

Mr. Johnstone escorted me into a building and to a room I would share with another girl. I cried for days, missing my grandparents, never seeing my brothers, desolate and afraid.

My roommate Elaine was older and had no sympathy for the wretch she was forced to tolerate. Exasperated, she proclaimed an end to my misery. "If you don't stop that, I'm going to make you. And you won't like it."

"I can't," I bawled, and continued to wail and sob. I imagined Billy's bewilderment now that we were separated. He would be lost without me, and I knew that part of myself had been amputated.

Her solution was to shove me into the closet and close the door. "Don't come out until you stop crying."

Imprisoned, I sat in the dark and wept. I was frightened and thought my world had ended, but even my despair could not deny the need to use the bathroom. Venturing out of confinement, I forced myself to be silent when Elaine was present. Every night I quietly cried myself to sleep.

THE HOME | 8

At home I had friends in church and school, and though Elaine and I had had a bad beginning, I did my best to get along with her. She exhibited no desire to be the friend of a weepy younger girl and took every opportunity to make my life miserable. I was only eight years old and no match for a bully. She teased me, threw my clothes on the floor, put toothpaste in my bed, and persecuted me whenever she could. Elaine's friends followed her example and shared the joy of tormenting the defenseless new arrival.

Administrators must have noticed Elaine's behavior, and to my relief, they moved her. My new roommate and I got along fine. A friend, however, could not be a substitute for my brothers.

I missed them both, especially Billy. He had always been my companion, my playmate, my responsibility, and in the strange new place I was sure he needed me more than ever. He and I had the same father and mother, making Billy my only full sibling. Though Tory had a different father and wasn't always with us, he was still my half-brother. After all, I was responsible for Billy and Tory being in that place, and I was not fulfilling my obligation to protect them.

The first week at the Stillbrook Christian Children's Home were the worst days of my life. Homesickness, guilt, and loneliness were my constant companions. I felt that we were in prison. No longer could I sit on our den sofa to snuggle next to Daisy and watch television. There was no one to hug and kiss me and show me I was special, until Daisy relied on the United States Postal Service. It was as if butterflies and flowers cascaded out of the envelopes, along with her love. I could endure my new world as long as Daisy still loved me.

Her letter told me all about her days since she left us. The little things like what she cooked for dinner and what the preacher said in his sermon. My heart soared. My grandparents hadn't deserted us! Daisy still loved me! I couldn't wait for her weekly letters, and the packages she sent every holiday. The candy, toys, and Crackerjacks were more than gifts, they were hugs in a box. Not as satisfying as a cuddle, but affirmation, nonetheless. Though I did not fully understand why we three were placed in the Home, my grandmother's constant communication bolstered my spirit and my crying decreased as I tried to adjust.

I occasionally caught glimpses of my brothers and were relieved to see them laughing and playing with friends. They waved to me and seemed happy, but if I had not been such a bad girl, if my grandparents had not discovered my secrets, the three of us would be safe at home with Daisy and Papaw. I feared that soon the adults at the Home would discover my secrets, too. They would make me leave. How could I protect my brothers then? After all, it was my fault they were there. Anguish, fear, and guilt dominated my thoughts, my dreams, my nightmares.

One Sunday about six months after arriving, I sat on the steps outside the chapel. Mr. Johnstone came to sit next to me. "Why are you crying, Abigail?"

"I miss my brothers," I cried. "I really miss them."

I wanted to see Tory, but it was Billy who was more than a brother to me. I could not remember when we had not been the most important person in each other's lives. It was almost as if the two of us comprised one being. "I need Billy," I sobbed. "He needs me, too."

Mr. Johnstone put his arm around my shoulder, and though he surely wanted to comfort me, I was frightened. Every time a man had paid attention to me, something bad happened. I didn't want the touching to begin again. Unsure what to expect, I shrank from him and cried even harder.

"You're going to be okay," he said as he stood. "Go back to your dorm and don't worry."

How could I not worry? My brothers were still so young, and though I was only eight, I was failing my self-imposed duty to care for them.

That caring man understood, and soon found a way to salve my anguish.

9 | ADJUSTING

Though the campus resembled a beautiful painting, I continued to view the Home as my prison.

As an adult, I now know that our grandparents did what they thought best for us and for themselves. They were in their late fifties and had raised their family. Three additional youngsters were too much for them. They put us in a well-run facility with well-intentioned people who administered important life skills and Christian values. The only element missing was love.

The Stillbrook, Kansas, facility was built on immaculately maintained wooded acreage of rolling hills and winding brooks. Stately red brick buildings with white columns and shutters were reminiscent of a college campus. Dormitories, administration building, gym, and church served the community of about 400 children. House parents lived in each dorm.

It was a strict but caring Christian environment. There were rules to be followed, manners to be learned, and chores to do. The goal was to cultivate personal growth and educational excellence. Competent counselors managed the students and encouraged activities to suit their interests and talents. Athletics, musical instruments, and voice lessons were available. Daily devotionals and weekly services insured our religious involvement, mine further supplemented by choir participation. Now as an adult, I know my years in the Children's Home helped mold my habits, developed my determination, and taught me to do right rather than wrong.

There was no mom to carpool us over the hundred acres of hilly terrain to reach our activities, church, or to catch the bus to public school. We walked. I trekked from my dorm up the first hill to reach the second hill. The route to the third hill dipped into a valley and crossed over a bridge bordered by a stone and rock wall. Because it was so deep in the valley and hidden from sight, teenagers named it sweetheart Bridge. I often took a break from the long walks to sit on the wall for a while, casting longing looks down into the inviting creek. I used the church's tall steeple as my compass and never was lost among the meandering paths and groves of trees.

Walking kept us fit and healthy, and established my lifelong habit. In later years I added jogging to my routine, which soon became running. When young, I ran free and joyous like the wind. Though now in my sixties my speed resembles a summer breeze. Nevertheless, I credit those activities with greatly aiding my mental and emotional recovery.

We children weren't isolated. Residents attended local public schools, and the Home provided tutors if needed. Unfortunately, the bus delivering us to our schools exhibited a logo boldly identifying our origin. All our classmates knew where we lived.

"Here come the orphans," they would chant as we disembarked.

"We're not orphans!"

"Your parents don't want you," someone would taunt.

"Do so!"

"If you don't live with your parents, you're just as good as orphans," another would tease.

Nobody at the Home was an orphan, but we didn't talk about where we came from. We didn't speak about our home life, parents, or anything that had happened to us. No one questioned the reason any of us were living at the Home instead of with our families. It didn't matter there; we were just kids engrossed in the business of growing up. We had so many activities, chores, and schoolwork that we never just sat down and talked.

I'm sure there were many like me who kept everything buried. We didn't have an outlet for our thoughts, our feelings, our fears, our tears. Anyway, whom would we tell? No therapists or mentors existed in those days. Most of the house parents were kind but were there for guidance and discipline. They didn't have time or show interest in hearing about our personal issues.

While most of the children wore donated garments from the Home's clothing room, my brothers and I proudly dressed in the finer clothes Daisy continued to purchase from the Roswell department store. Since all our washing was handled in the Home's commercial laundry, it was necessary to identify whose was whose. When we changed into gym clothes in school, the names written inside our garments were exposed, generating snickers and scornful taunts hurled at us defenseless Stillbrook residents. Each dart jabbed at my heart.

The teasing and derision were embarrassing, but if those bullies knew what my mother did to me, they would realize I needed to be safely away from her. My best defense was to ignore the tormentors and not let it bother me. I was good at burying my feelings, a skill which has served me well throughout my life.

My brothers resided in a boys' dorm and I in a girls', each housing up to 35 children. Our house parents regimented our schedule from 5:00 a.m. wakeup to bedtime according to our ages. Everyone did their dormitory chores on a rotating basis. We cleaned the common areas, kept the magnificent wood floors polished to a high shine, and cooked our meals. We learned to pass food to the right, the dish changing hands to travel around the table in the proper way even if the person requesting the dish was sitting on your left. Please, thank you, ma'am and sir became second nature. Though the rules were strict, our lives were good. We were safe and secure, with a roof over our heads, enough to eat, and clean clothes to wear.

My only grievance was the absence of my brothers. Though I saw Billy on the bus to school and in church, the hole in my heart needed him. About two weeks after Mr. Johnstone had spent a moment with me on the chapel steps, my house mother came to my room.

"Let me help you pack your things."

I was confused, but immediately thought that Mr. Johnstone had finally discovered my secret and was sending me away. I was too frightened to ask where I was going or if Billy and Tory would be with me.

"I know you miss your brothers, Abby," she said as she emptied my few drawers. "You three will be together."

Thanks to the kind Mr. Johnstone, we moved into the newest and loveliest building at the Home, a dormitory for brothers and sisters. What a wonderful surprise. The dorm parents were a sweet couple who became my surrogate grandparents. It would have been a blissful existence if Tory didn't find trouble as often as he could.

TROUBLE | 10

Billy did his best, and so did I, but we had no influence on Tory. We frequently heard that our brother was grounded or had his head shaved in punishment.

"Why is Tory always in trouble?" Billy asked me in frustration. "He won't listen when I tell him to behave."

I knew his problem. "Tory didn't have Daisy and Papaw," I said. "He needed more time with them."

Billy didn't answer at first, but I could see him processing that idea. "And he didn't have Mama Faye, either."

"We're lucky, Billy," I said. "Daisy and Mama Faye were better than our real mother."

Billy squinted as he thought about that. "I guess Barbara isn't a very good mother for Tory, either."

"She lets him do anything he wants, like she does." I shuddered to think of all she wanted to do to me.

Billy shook his head. "If he does anything he wants, why is he so angry all the time?"

I thought about that. "I don't think Barbara loves him."

I realized another probability. "Tory probably knows that."

Billy nodded his agreement. "She doesn't love us, either."

"Maybe she doesn't love you or Tory, but she hates me."

Billy didn't answer. Instead, he said, "I wish I could keep him out of trouble."

That was a safer topic. "So do I," I said, "but Tory looks for trouble. We just have to take care of ourselves."

"But everybody knows he's my brother," Billy complained. "They tease me when he gets caught."

"It's easy to know when he did something bad," I said. "You just need to see his head."

"Tory is always bald," Billy sighed. "I think he's proud of it."

Despite the burden of our young brother, those were good times for Billy and me. We adjusted to the routine. We got to know all the children at the Home, were involved in sports and music, and did well in school. Though I was happy there, I still missed my church, my home, and even my Aunt Joyce.

Thankfully, our grandparents showed their love in enough ways to sustain me. Billy and I lived for Daisy's weekly letters, and through them felt valued despite our lives far away from her. She and Papaw drove to Stillbrook twice a year and took us away for a weekend. The hugs and kisses my grandmother showered upon me provided joy for months. Even Papaw seemed to pay a little attention to us on those trips.

I cherished the visits with my grandparents but dreaded the times Barbara showed up. She checked into a rundown hotel nearby and we had to stay with her. Tory was even more wild on those few days, while Billy and I stuck together and quietly did our homework. We thought his tantrums and annoying behavior were intended for Barbara to notice him, but our mother smoked and drank beer and talked on the phone. She paid little attention to her children. I stayed as close to Billy as I could, fearing she would find a way to indulge in our secret. I think we all, including Barbara, were relieved when the weekends ended, and she left us in front of our dormitory.

For a long time, Barbara didn't come to see us. Daisy never said anything about our mother in her weekly letters. I tried not to think about Barbara and the despicable things she did to me, but Billy was curious. Why didn't she even come to see Tory? Had there been an accident? Was she sick?

"Stop pestering me," I told Billy. "I'll write Daisy and ask." My grandmother's answering letter was a surprise.

Your mother has married again and moved far away, too far to visit you and your brothers. Don't expect to see her any time soon. Always know that Papaw and I love you.

Billy was disappointed that our mother couldn't visit us, and I was happy that she was too far to affect me. We learned that the new husband's name was David. Like all her previous relationships, it didn't last. Daisy wrote that Barbara was back in Roswell with Papaw and her. I dreaded more visits, but she didn't bother to come see her children.

One day I read exciting news in my grandmother's weekly letter and ran to find Billy. "Daisy and Papaw are coming here next Saturday!"

"But it isn't time yet," he said. "They just came last month."

Breathless, I showed him the letter. "Tory's grandparents are coming to see him. Daisy and Papaw want to meet them."

Barbara didn't accompany them. I couldn't help being jealous that Tory had more family than we did. We had no idea where our own father was nor who were his people. They have never been part of our lives. But we were happy that we could see our grandparents again so soon. Tory's family were very nice to bring presents to Billy and me, too, and our rebellious brother was on his best behavior. Of course, that lasted only as long as the visit.

One day, our dorm mother found Billy and me on our way to the school bus. "You two need to stay home today."

"Why?" I had prepared for a test and was afraid the teacher would give me a bad grade if I missed it.

She sighed. "It's Tory." Her worried look frightened me, and I urged her to tell us what was going on. "He's run away. Two of his friends went with him."

We waited for more information, but she began to cry. So did I. "It must be bad," I said tearfully.

She shook her head as she delivered the frightening news. "A boy has drowned." She blew her nose before adding, "We don't know which one."

Billy and I waited, fearful that our incorrigible brother had met his end. I never understood why the adults put us children through that anxiety before knowing the outcome. Though greatly relieved to learn that the victim was not our brother, I was angry with Tory for acting as if rules didn't apply to him. In truth, he was just like our mother. Tory thought he could do what he wanted, without regard for the burden he placed on everyone else.

The Home refused to deal with Tory any longer. Barbara took her wayward son and left Billy and me behind. I moved to a girls' dorm and Billy to a boys'. They were in better locations on campus, and I was happy that I didn't have to walk as far to meet the school bus. We had adjusted to life at the Home, and I felt protected from the woman who had abused me. It was a safe period in my life, a time of security and stability.

11 | ANOTHER HOME

A few months after Tory left, our dorm mothers told Billy and me to pack our clothes. "You're going home," Mrs. Roland said. I was very excited to return to Daisy and Papaw, until I heard the plan. "Your mother is coming to pick you up."

"You mean my grandmother?"

"No, your mother. She'll be here soon. Don't leave anything behind."

Why were we going with Barbara? Billy and I were even more surprised to hear that she had married again. Jim was her fifth husband, though we were never sure she married every man she lived with or who had fathered her children. They had bought a house and we were going to live with them and Tory.

"Now we'll have a daddy," Billy said hopefully.

"Maybe." My experiences with men had been frightening. I did not look forward to living with the woman who subjected me to that abuse. Nor did I want a man so close.

Billy couldn't drop the subject. "Tory has his own

daddy," he said. "Maybe Jim will like us. I'll ask him to be ours."

I didn't want to have anything to do with a man. "Just because we don't know our daddy, we don't need Jim. We have Papaw."

Billy shook his head. We both knew our grumpy grandfather was not a substitute father.

We moved into their house, and I found Jim to be very quiet. I didn't know if our mother was working or just out and about, but she was never home. Jim became our caregiver. Billy and I discussed our new situation.

"Jim's weird, right?" Billy asked.

"We never had a daddy, so how would we know what he's supposed to be like?"

"I guess we don't," Billy said. "But I'm glad we don't have so many rules here."

I agreed and liked a new habit Jim introduced to us. He loved to read, and on Sundays, he would take us to a bookstore and purchase the latest best sellers. He treated us to comics. We all spent the afternoon enthralled with our stories.

But sometimes Jim was at work and the boys were at their friends' houses or participating in sports. When my mother happened to be home, my worst fears were realized. There was no escape.

"Come with me, Abigail," she directed. We went to her

bedroom, or mine, or even to the living room sofa. I had to do what she commanded; she did to me what she wished.

No entreaties or tears stopped her from taking vile liberties, nor from telling me how bad I was. My previous fear that I would be sent away was now replaced with hope that I could go back to the Home. Those thoughts filled me with guilt that I would then be unable to protect Billy from her filthy attentions.

Barbara's verbal abuse escalated as I entered puberty and began to develop. "You're ugly, Abigail. You'll never find a husband."

My body was changing into a woman's shape, showing signs of the same slim figure, small waist, and full bust as Barbara's. I did not understand any of that abusive language. "But you always told me I was pretty. You said my hair was so beautiful."

Her repeated comments took root in my mind. I believed her.

"You're not pretty now," she sneered. "You'll never make a man happy. You'll never get married."

Her verbal abuse was as devastating as the physical liberties she inflicted on my body and soul. I believed no one could possibly want or like me. Keeping vile secrets, I concealed the truth of what I was and what was happening to me. If only I had had the courage to confide in someone, my life would have been different.

My only hope of winning my mother's love and making friends was to become an overachiever. I thought that if I could play piano, violin, and flute, sing well in the choir, and excel in school, my secrets would be buried. I would be safe.

Living with my family didn't fulfill the dreams I had nurtured in the Home. Constant anxiety and determination to earn praise occupied my every thought. If I could prove to Barbara that I was a good person, that I was valuable, perhaps she would see that her abuse was unwarranted. I would do anything to gain her approval.

But she found fault in everything I said or did. Though I was an outstanding student, she berated me for occasional less than perfect grades. She suddenly moved my brothers and me from public elementary school to a Catholic school. I didn't know why because we weren't Catholics. It was a greater distance from our house. Someone had to drive us.

A few of the nuns were nice, but others were unreasonably strict.

"Your letters are not correct, Abigail," the nun said as she frequently slapped my knuckles with a ruler. I tried to slant them to the right, but I was a left-handed writer. It was impossible to please her.

"Why do I have to go?" I asked my mother. "The nun is so mean, and I hate all that kneeling and bending." I complained that I had to sit quietly and wait while the Catholic students went up to the front for communion. I was in the choir and was often obligated to sing at funerals and endure an unfamiliar service. Again I was the outsider with no friends. I didn't understand why I had to attend that school.

She scoffed at my pleas to return to the neighborhood elementary. "You're a bad girl, Abigail. The nuns know what to do with bad girls."

I wasn't perfect, but seldom got into trouble except with my mother. My futile efforts to be good were never rewarded.

Barbara had various jobs and often worked nights, coming home after we were asleep. One morning she refused to wake up to drive us to school, and I had to be there for a test. "I have to leave, Billy. Do you want to come with me?"

"It's too far," he said.

"I don't care. I'll get into trouble if I don't take the test."

I walked. It took me most of the day. The Father saw a bedraggled, hungry eleven-year-old enter the school. "What happened, Abigail?"

"I walked. Can I take the test now?"

I didn't get into trouble, but apparently some phone calls took place. The next day Jim took Billy and me back to the Stillbrook Christian Children's Home.

"Why can't we live with Daisy and Papaw?" I asked him.

"Why does Tory get to stay?" Billy asked. "Why is he special?"

Jim remained stoic and silent as he drove us to the Home, leaving us to wonder why our lives were so unfair. How could our mother do such horrible things to me? Why did she send Billy and me away, yet love Tory and want to keep him? Despite his incorrigible behavior, Tory had no limits and suffered no reckoning, while Billy and I could do no right. We were supposed to love and honor our mother, but there was no commandment for a parent to do the same for all their children. The two of us meant nothing to her. We only knew love because of Daisy.

Billy and I always kept in touch with Tory and tried to accept that it was not his fault our mother favored him. However, our animosity toward the undeserving boy who was loved and preferred over us has remained throughout our lives.

12 | SUMMER BUS

Though Billy and I were back in the Home, our grandparents didn't forget us. As we reached our preteen years, they sent bus tickets. We didn't get to go home for Christmas, but Billy and I visited them in Roswell during the summer and for spring break. Between visits, I relived those special intervals in my dreams, and eagerly looked forward to the next time.

For a special treat when we were younger, Daisy would fry up chicken. It was so much better than the Home's version. Sometimes we would take the motor coach to the lake and camp there overnight. The Murdock boys were our constant companions, their mischief getting all us kids into trouble. It was great fun when we were in Roswell.

If our Uncle Brent was home from Divinity School, he would drive us around town and to the lake. Once he took us to Saint Louis to see the house Mama Faye and Papa Will had owned. It was a rare treat when Aunt Joyce and I did girl things together. She sometimes put makeup on me or tried to tame my unruly curls. For me, my real home was always Roswell, threatened only by my secrets. I feared the moments Barbara came to get me. My grandmother believed our times together established a bond. She seemed to have no idea what I endured.

"Come on, Abigail," Barbara would say as she breezed into the big house. "Pack a bag."

I had to accompany her to wherever she was living at the time. If I refused, Daisy would ask questions I dared not answer. Sometimes, it seemed a man lived with her, and other times, men came and went. I never knew if men's clothes and toiletries would be present, but when she brought me to her home, a man usually showed up.

She made a pallet for me on the floor next to her bed. Occasionally, I spent the night and slept there, but even for daytime visits, she ordered me to lie on the pallet. Often a man would come to her on her bed.

"Just be still, Abigail," she told me. "Stay on your bed." I was too frightened to disobey. I thought I had no choice. Their moans, their movements, their words rang in my ears, and I sobbed quietly, knowing not to disturb them.

When the man left, my mother proceeded to destroy me with her comments. "This is something you'll never have, Abigail. No man will ever love you." Everything I observed and heard seemed nasty and disgusting, and I didn't want to be loved by a man. I kept my secrets deep and safe to earn the only love important to me: my grandmother's.

Why did I submit to her directives? I was governed by fear of losing Daisy's love, an irrational belief fomented by a sick woman. If only I had sought help, an advocate. But I relied on myself to endure the hell my mother created for me.

When she chose to focus her attention on me, I learned to go to other places in my mind. I'd see the lake and the waves, and people running, having fun. I'd visualize mountains. I always loved nature, so I escaped to the most beautiful places I could imagine. I pretended the activity going on above me was not happening. I went to my happy place where I couldn't feel or know or participate.

As my body matured and hormones flowed, it became harder to transcend Barbara's ministrations by finding my happy place. The touching began to feel good. I couldn't justify the pleasure I experienced because I knew it was wrong. I felt guilty and dirty and bad. As conflicted as I was, suicide never occurred to me. My Christian faith taught that committing suicide sent one straight to hell. I prayed God would forgive me my sins and allow me into Heaven.

As much as I treasured the good times when visiting Roswell, my secrets kept me fearful. It was a relief to board the bus back to Stillbrook. I could forget the vile sessions with my mother as Billy and I spent the time recounting the fun of the visit. I was about fourteen when I saw a familiar face already on board. "Hi Opal," I said to the girl sitting quietly by a window. "I didn't know you lived in Illinois, too."

She shyly smiled, head down as she crinkled her shirt hem in her fingers. "It's just a little town," she said. "Eastwood."

I shook my head. "Never heard of it."

Still toying with her hem, she said, "My uncle is stationed at Scott Air Force base." When I didn't comment, she explained. "Mostly military people live there."

"The base must be close." She nodded and I asked, "Okay if I sit by you?"

She nodded again. I put my backpack in the overhead rack and my lunch sack on the aisle seat while Billy claimed the vacant one across from me. All the kids at the Home knew each other, but I was a little older than Opal and we had not spent any time together. No one talked about our lives before coming to the Home, but I was curious. We had a two-hour ride for my bold questions. This was unfamiliar ground for both of us.

"So, you were visiting your uncle?"

"Yes." Opal's shirt hem was now so creased only an iron could smooth it.

"Billy and I stayed with our grandparents." She didn't answer, so I continued. "Daisy is really more like our mother."

Opal turned to look at me, eyes questioning. "Don't you have a mother?" She quickly lowered her head as her fingers resumed their action.

I couldn't escape the truth. "Yes, but we don't see her much."

"She doesn't act like a mother," Billy interjected, "and we don't have a daddy." He saw Opal's furrowed brow and added, "Daisy and Papaw take care of us."

"What about you, Opal?" I asked, moving the

conversation away from our own family. "Do you have a mother and father?"

Her long silence signaled my blunder.

"I'm sorry," I said. "You don't have to tell me if you don't want to."

"Okay."

Maybe I wasn't the only one with secrets. Searching for a different topic, I ventured another question. "So, did you stay in Eastwood all summer? We only spent two weeks in Roswell."

"Just a week," she said, "but I had fun with my cousins." Opal seemed to relax as I told her about our summer activities and our adventures with the Murdock brothers. I learned she liked to sing and encouraged her to join the church choir. When she came with me to the first practice of the new school year, I knew I had made a friend.

"You have a beautiful voice," I said on our walk back to our dorm. "I think Pastor Goodman was impressed."

She smiled. "I never wanted anyone to hear me sing."

"Whyever not?"

"My daddy made fun of me. Said I sounded like a squeaky mouse."

"How awful! No wonder you didn't sing before now."

We walked in silence until we reached sweetheart Bridge, then sat on the rock wall and rested. Opal spoke up.

"Anyway, I was always so tired."

"I don't know what you mean," I said.

"I didn't sing much. Just wanted to sleep all the time."

That didn't make sense to me. "When?"

"When I lived with my parents."

"Were you sick?"

"I don't know."

I thought about that remark as we resumed our walk. "Did you have to stay in bed?"

"No, I just felt like I was dreaming." She turned to look at me. "All the time it was like I was sleepwalking."

"Like in school? At home?"

"All the time."

I stopped walking and put my hand on her shoulder. "Do you feel that way now?"

"Not anymore. That's why I live here at the Home."

"Opal, you have to tell me what you're talking about."

"This lady came to our house one day and took me. The next day they gave me to my aunt and uncle. They have four kids already, so they brought me here."

We sat on a bench outside our dorm and Opal told me more. "My daddy gave me pills, and sometimes my mom had to take them, too."

"What were they for?"

"I'm not sure, but I wasn't so scared when I took them."

"Scared of what?"

"Daddy."

I understood fear. I didn't need to know what her daddy did to frighten her, and why he gave her pills. I certainly did not want to reveal my own secrets. Instead, I perfected my façade to hide the dirty, ugly, unlovable girl behind the mask. I now knew another girl like me.

"You're safe here, Opal. We're all safe here."

It was good to have a friend. Our dormitory mother assigned us together, and chores were easier working in tandem. Always Billy's sibling, friend, and protector, I naturally assumed the same role for Opal. Though the two knew nothing of my secret life, they each provided stability and distraction from my fears. They needed me and I needed them.

BILLY | 13

At first, I thought that our family had abandoned Billy and me to life in a prison, but our grandparents had done what was best for us. Our mom was out of our lives for several years, and we neither saw nor heard from her. Because our grandparents visited us in Stillbrook a few times a year and brought us to Roswell, as well, we knew we were loved.

Billy thrived. Naturally athletic, my brother was also gregarious and well-liked. His roommates and dorm brothers viewed him as their leader, and his successful adjustment to life in the Home lessened my guilt. We grew up in a wholesome environment without fear. Life was good then for us.

The Home published a magazine every month to show donors that their money was being spent for a good cause. The publisher photographed our activities and wrote articles to encourage contributions.

He showcased our choir practice for an issue and noticed me. "What's your name?"

"Abigail."

"You're very photogenic, Abigail." He pointed to my greatest asset, which was also my inescapable curse. "That blonde curly hair stands out." I didn't know what to say. "What other activities interest you?"

I mentioned the sports I liked and the musical instruments I was learning to play. He frequently featured those topics in subsequent issues and photographed me. For the first time in my life, a man who was not a relative treated me with respect. I was wary but not afraid. We chatted about my interests, and he encouraged me to pursue my goals. Knowing that I wanted to become a news announcer, he often picked me up after school and drove me to a local television station, where I learned about broadcasting. He put me in front of the camera, and I would proudly smile and point at the scores posted. He was my first mentor, though I didn't know the word then.

"Hey Abby," the kids taunted, "we saw you on TV again." Then they would pose and point and fluff their nonexistent curls. Their teasing meant nothing to me. It was only my mother's approval that mattered. I hoped that she heard about my achievements and was proud of me, but I had no way of knowing. We had no communication.

I thrived in the safety of structure and routine, but Billy developed differently. As a teen, he grew more self-confident and thus defiant of the rules that were good for me. His escapades involved sneaking away from the campus with other rebellious boys, then during class sleeping off the previous night's drinking. Billy yielded to temptation once too often and was expelled. Barbara had already divested herself of him, but reluctantly took him back to Roswell to live with Jim, Tory, and herself.

Daisy's letters told me that as a duo, my two brothers got into more mischief than ever. Even though at the Home I had not been able to keep Billy out of trouble, guilt overwhelmed me. Believing our grandparents had sent us away because they knew my secrets, I was convinced Billy would have behaved appropriately if we lived under their care instead of with our mother or in Stillbrook. My precocious, fun-loving brother had become incorrigible, and it was my fault. I missed him terribly.

There was only one solution. I wrote Barbara and begged to return and live with them. Billy needed me.

Once again, the dorm mother informed me that I should pack my things. My stepfather Jim picked me up and drove me to Roswell, to my self-imposed Purgatory. I was prepared to endure my mother's abuse for the greater good of helping Billy become a more responsible young man. I tried, but her sexual and emotional abuse escalated and was too much for me to bear. I called the Administrator of the Stillbrook Christian Home.

"It's Abigail," I managed to say before I began sobbing.

"How are you, dear?"

I couldn't speak. The reason for my call was obvious.

"I'll be there tomorrow," he said. "First, I need to speak with your mother, but don't worry, Abby. We always have a place for you."

I was relieved to be back, and accepted my life as it was.

I now knew the Home was the safest place for me. Though I didn't develop close relationships with many, the kids I grew up with were there. It was familiar. It was home.

Barbara's abuse had made me afraid to trust. Most relationships were hard for me, though I felt comfortable with the Administrator and my house parents. Always well behaved, I felt safest staying to myself, making few friends. I didn't follow the crowd. Content to keep active and busy, I rarely got into mischief.

Several weeks after my return, my friend Opal found me in the dorm kitchen peeling potatoes for dinner. "Abby, Billy is here." She handed me a note.

"I don't understand. How could he be in Stillbrook?"

"I saw him getting out of a yellow Volkswagen bug. He told me to find you and give you this."

"That's our mom's car," I said incredulously as I revealed the message to her. "Tory and Billy are waiting for me by the river in the park."

Opal's eyes widened at the implications of their presence. "Are they old enough to drive? Do you think your mother knows they're here?"

"Absolutely not!" My brothers had done it again, but I was too excited to care. I ran to find our dorm mother for permission to meet them.

"How nice of your family to pay a surprise visit," she said. I had conveniently omitted the information that it was only my young brothers who had made the trip. It took me fifteen minutes to run to them at the river.

Fifteen-year-old Billy had grown taller and handsomer in that short interval, and I couldn't resist ruffling his unruly hair. He laughingly did the same to mine and we hugged with enthusiasm. Tory and I joyously greeted each other, too, and my brothers told me their astonishing story.

"I miss you, Abby," Billy said, "but Mom wouldn't take me to see you."

Tory jumped in. "So we took her keys and some money and here we are." His triumphant grin was contagious, but I needed to know more.

"How did y'all know about shifting gears? Or which roads to take?" I turned to Tory. "You're only thirteen, you idiot. Could you even see over the steering wheel?"

"Aren't you glad to see us, Abby?" Billy's big smile disarmed me.

"Of course I am," I laughed, "but you're lucky a cop didn't stop you."

Before I had to return and serve dinner, we spent a joyful hour chattering and laughing. I ran back to my dorm, laughing at the thought of their big adventure, and the consequences when they returned Barbara's car.

In Daisy's next letter I learned that the surprise visit had ended catastrophically. The truants were tired after their long drive from Roswell to Stillbrook and the adrenalin effects of surprising me had worn off. They napped in the car before leaving the park after dark. Recent heavy rains had washed out part of the river embankment, and Tory's inability to see over the steering wheel kept him from noticing the hazard. If a tree hadn't stopped the car's descent into the river, they might have drowned. As it was, the fire department came to rescue them. The car was totaled, and our stepfather had to drive to Stillbrook and retrieve them.

As usual, our mother forgave Tory and punished Billy, sending him to a boys' home near Roswell. Aunt Joyce had never visited us in Stillbrook, but when Billy was so close to her, she occasionally brought him gifts. In later years she told me she always felt guilty that we were placed in care. I wonder if she would have helped me if I had confided in her.

Billy only stayed in that Home for six months. After returning to Roswell to live with our grandparents, he enrolled in a high school program to train as a mechanic. He never again got into trouble, though he has battled alcoholism all his life and was involved in several accidents driving under its influence. He and I have spent our lives facing our demons.

HARDY | 14

In March of 1972, I went back to Roswell and joined Billy at the big house to stay with our grandparents for spring break. I noticed that our teenage exuberance disrupted their quiet home routine. Daisy encouraged us to hang out with our neighbors, the Murdock boys, and that was fine with Billy and me. We had spent many happy hours roaming the neighborhood with them. I relished those short bursts of normalcy, imagining a life lived with my family instead of in an institution.

During that visit, I met Justin, a mechanic in the garage where Billy trained, and he took an interest in me. We went to a movie, and another time we sat on the swings in my grandparents' yard and talked for a long while. Though I knew boys became men who did the things Barbara's men did, I was attracted to Justin. I was seventeen and believed that I could ignore my secrets and be a normal teenager.

Unlike Justin, the Murdocks were like my brothers, and we regularly walked together to the neighborhood store for our daily snack supply. One day we noticed that there was a new boy sacking groceries. He was older than us, and we had never seen him before. Bond Murdock looked at me and said, "Man, y'all could be related."

His brother Hicks whistled in agreement. Sure enough, that boy had a gorgeous head of blonde curly hair. It was just like Billy's and mine. Of course, he overheard and grinned at me. When he sacked our order and moved to carry it out for us, Bond took the bag away from him. That was the first inkling I had that my neighbor kind of liked me. I was fully developed, and boys were starting to interest me. My active hormones helped me suppress my fear. The grocery boy seemed nice, though, and I thought he was cute.

"What's your name?" he asked.

I told him.

I thought about him that afternoon and walked back to the grocery to see if he was still there. He saw me and smiled. "Hi, Abigail. Good to see you again."

"You know my name, but I don't know yours."

"It's Hardy. Short for Hardeman Cooper Wells, Junior."

"Nice to meet you, Hardy."

"You want to go to a movie with me?"

I did, and a few days later he came to pick me up for the Wednesday matinee at the theater next to the grocery store. Billy and Tory were at the Murdocks, and Papaw was at work. When we heard Hardy's knock, I waited in the den while my grandmother answered the door. I noticed she paused for a long while before escorting him to me.

"Abby, is this the young man you told me about?"

Of course, he was. Why else would he have come to our

house? Puzzled, I nodded. She asked his name. Her gasp surprised me.

"Kids, I need y'all to sit down." My grandmother took a deep breath and sat on a chair as we tenuously took seats on the couch. She looked at Hardy and then at me. "I'm not sure how to tell you this."

I held my breath. I had never seen Daisy seem so hesitant to speak. "What is it, Daisy?" I asked. "Are you sick?"

She shook her head and with a deep breath, squared her shoulders as if to prepare herself. Perplexed, I waited for an explanation. "Abigail," she said to me, then turned to face Hardy. I sensed him sitting straighter, waiting as I did for the bombshell that was surely coming. "Children, you are brother and sister."

He and I were speechless. Daisy began crying so pitifully that I didn't want to make her feel worse. There was too much to comprehend and no way for me to understand what was happening. Both Hardy and I remained silent until she gained a bit of control.

Taking his hand, she said in a shaking voice, "Hardy, I'm your grandmother."

Hardy let out a whoop and hugged her. I was stunned when he said, "I moved to Roswell to find my family."

We never made it to the movie.

"I was adopted," he said, "and always knew my mother came from here."

It was as if the dam had broken. The information flowed as never before. Daisy told us about her daughter, revealing facts previously hidden from me. Barbara was barely out of high school when she met Sergeant Hardeman Wells. Stationed at the nearby military base, he was dashing in his uniform and told exciting tales of his overseas deployments. When she became pregnant, the couple planned to drive all the way to Mexico where an underage girl didn't require parental approval to marry. Though devastated that their daughter had sinned, my grandparents acknowledged that the couple should marry in Illinois instead. They would legitimize their child as a United States citizen. The newlyweds lived on the base with their baby, and Barbara remained there when her husband deployed overseas again. He returned a year later to find his wife pregnant with me.

"I don't care who the father is," the sergeant said to his wife. "I'll raise both the children as my own."

A year of separation had changed her feelings. Barbara now loved my father, Lieutenant William Paxton. She insisted on a divorce from Hardeman.

"I'll agree on one condition," he proposed to the woman who had broken his heart. "Give me full custody of our son." Hardeman didn't ask who my father was.

Hardy grew up with his father and stepmother, and never discovered Barbara until he met me. I now knew I had three brothers, each named after his father. Hardeman Cooper Wells, Junior. William David Paxton, Junior. Victor Armstrong Sidell, Junior. Hardy, Billy, and Tory.

Daisy stood. "You kids wait here. I'm going to call Barbara."

I dutifully remained on the sofa near Hardy, silently fidgeting, confused and frightened. What could I say to a brother I just met? Was there no limit to Barbara's secrets?

"Your mother is so happy you're here, Hardy," Daisy said, "and she wants you two to come see her."

"Why me?" I asked. I had purposefully avoided Barbara during that spring break trip, and it had been a gloriously carefree visit. The last person I wanted to see now was my mother. It had been months since I had had contact with her and did not know where she was living or working or if she was involved with a man. But Daisy seemed happy that her wayward daughter would now meet her firstborn.

"Your mom will be waiting in a motel near here. Bring your swimming suit, Abby, because there's a pool, and Hardy can borrow Billy's. It'll be fun getting to know each other." I thought my grandmother seemed to be grasping for positive things to say to two kids who were dumbfounded. I listened as she continued her uncharacteristic remarks. "Hardy can tell you all about how he grew up, and you can tell him about the Home."

Over the years, I always wondered about that day. If the boys had not been at our neighbors', would they have gone with me and Hardy to see our mom? Would that have changed the outcome of the day? But they weren't there.

Hardy drove us to the seedy part of town and found the shabby motel. Mom was standing on the sidewalk of the parking lot, waving to us. She had on shorts and a halter top, and I wondered why she wasn't wearing a swimsuit if we were going into the pool.

Hardy parked and hesitantly approached the mother he never knew. They looked at each other for several moments, and I knew they saw the obvious resemblance among the three of us. Mom shook her head as she scrutinized his face. "Well, you look like him, too." She ruffled his blonde curls and laughed. "You two kids are peas in a pod." Barbara was right. We could be twins.

She walked away, saying, "I'll find some towels while you get in the pool."

Still amazed at the situation, I silently followed Hardy into the water. "I'm guessing this is all news to you," he said.

"I had no idea about you."

"Why don't we just get to know each other," he smiled. "You're my new sister."

"I guess so," I agreed. My brother and I spent the next few hours at the pool with our mother, conversing about the separate lives we had led and the families who had raised us. I buried my secrets and pretended they didn't exist. Throughout the day, Hardy and I kept eyeing each other, still marveling because we looked so much alike, even though we had different fathers. Blue eyes, curly blonde hair, fair skin. We frolicked and splashed in the pool, and I felt that I was making a new friend.

After a few hours, we were getting hungry. "Come with me," our mother said. "I made some sandwiches."

In her room I saw her clothes and toiletries strewn about. Nothing indicated a man was staying there with her. I didn't know if she lived in that motel or was just there to meet

Hardy. We devoured the bologna and cheese sandwiches and potato chips, and thirstily drank lemonade. I had rarely eaten a meal prepared by my mother. We returned to the pool after lunch, carefree and enjoying the glorious experience with a woman who was nothing like the mother I had come to fear and hate.

"Y'all hear that?" We knew the thunder was a storm warning, and it was time to go inside. I went toward the bathroom to change out of my bikini, drying off on the way.

"Stop, Abby," Barbara said.

I turned to see what she meant.

She motioned to me. "Sit on the bed." Mom pointed to my brother. "You too, Hardy."

"I want to talk to y'all." Hardy and I looked at each other, eyes wide in questioning surprise. Hadn't we been talking all day?

"So y'all like each other, huh?"

Since she was looking at me, I answered. "He's my brother, so I guess I do."

Then Barbara took a step to the little table by the window and closed the curtains. She sat in the nearby wooden chair and reached to open the drawer. Curious and unsuspecting, Hardy and I watched as she picked up the gun she must have hidden there.

I couldn't believe my eyes. My grandparents didn't have guns. I had never seen a real one, and though the weapon was small, I was frightened. She waved it, unsteadily pointing to each of us as she began giving orders.

"Stand up, Abby." I did. "Take off your swimsuit."

Hardy stood up. "I'm sorry," he said. "I'll leave. Give you privacy."

She pointed the gun at him. "Sit down."

The mother I knew had returned. Crying, I murmured "No, no." He did what she demanded as I sobbed.

She pointed her finger at me. "Take off your top!"

My mother's wickedness had escalated to sickness. How could she treat her daughter with such hate and disregard? Trying not to vomit, I turned my back to Hardy.

"Turn around!"

I expected her to shoot me. Crying and shaking, I nevertheless stood frozen in place.

"I said take off that top!"

Relenting, I kept my back to Hardy and untied the bikini. Despite my embarrassment, I didn't want to die. When she again ordered me to turn around, I followed her instructions to take off the bottoms. Hardy watched as commanded, now crying as desperately as I.

"Sit on the chair, Abby."

It was cold and hard, like my mother's hatred of me. I wrapped my arms around my chest, partly for warmth but mostly out of shame. I tried to summon the escape I had perfected from the age of four, but my mind would not take me away, would not send me soaring into another world while the evil was happening to me in this one.

I wanted to die then, and since that moment I wish she had shot me. I would not have to relive the horror that came next. The rest of my life was defined by that day.

15 | THE HAUNTING

Nothing Barbara had done to me, nothing I had endured, no amount of guilt or anguish I suffered, prepared me for the experience of that afternoon. The memories still haunt me. Yet years of therapy have helped me accept that I am who I am today because of that day. And despite that day. The scene returns again and again, and I see myself sitting on the chair, shivering and naked as my mother directed an act straight from hell.

"Touch her breasts," she said to Hardy, now clearly slurring her words. When had she become inebriated? "Hold them. Squeeze them."

He closed his eyes as he followed her commands, while I sobbed and looked anywhere but at him or Barbara.

"I need Abby to get on the bed now."

I burrowed under the covers, but that wouldn't do. She threw the blanket and sheet on the floor and continued her macabre plot.

"It's your turn," she sneered at the miserably sobbing boy and pointed to his swimsuit.

My mother had abused me for years, but I did not expect that. This behavior was different from any other I had experienced, and I knew her erratic and unpredictable conduct would end disastrously. I wish I had been wrong.

"On second thought," she said, "take it off real slow." She watched Hardy's progress with hunger, moving to touch him as he lowered his swimsuit. "You're going to get to know your sister real well," she said with a lascivious grin. Then she hovered over me as I lay crying on the bed. "And you, little lady, are going to learn what being a sister is all about."

I've thought about that remark many times over the years. Had her older brother abused her? Uncle Mark was already living away from the family when Billy and I arrived. Had my mother's evil been inspired by her own experience?

Naked and crying, both Hardy and I were frightened of her as she carelessly waved the gun. We did as we were told. "I want to see how much y'all like each other," she said as her breathing quickened. "Get on top of her," she motioned to Hardy. "I bet you've done this before." Her drunken laughter matched the volume of our sobs.

Lying on a pallet by Barbara's bed, I had listened to her and various men as they engaged in intercourse. The moans, the grunts, the breathless dialogue, and the frantic movements were familiar to me. I knew which body parts fit together, and I had felt pleasure and wetness as their passion excited me, too. But I had never lain with a man.

Two years older than I, Hardy knew what to do. As

Barbara brandished her gun and sipped from a flask, he followed her direction. I shrieked in pain when he penetrated my maidenhood. Barbara laughed and encouraged him to move faster and push harder, as I screamed. Though the event seemed to me to last hours, it couldn't have been more than five minutes when Hardy relaxed and removed his flaccid penis from me.

I felt so dirty, I wanted to die.

Why did we submit? Though one of us might have been shot, it was unlikely we would be killed. We could have overpowered her. Hardy seemed stunned by her behavior and didn't react, and I was accustomed to yielding to her demands. Our secrets became even more vile as that evil woman infused her poison into both Hardy and me.

With the conclusion of the scene she had directed, Barbara stood and said, "Now y'all have been properly introduced."

NEVER OVER | 16

When it was over, our mother just walked out of the room and left us alone. I wrapped myself with the bedding Hardy picked up from the floor, both of us avoiding speaking or making eye contact. Buried under the covers, I sobbed in devastation while he cleaned himself in the tiny bathroom. My tenuous world had crashed. My secrets would now be too overwhelming to hide.

When Hardy had dressed, our mother returned and calmly addressed him. "You will never tell anyone about this day." The threat was worse than I expected. "If you do, it's Abigail who will pay for it."

Hardy's eyes widened in disbelief, but I knew that she meant to make my fear and guilt even more agonizing.

Barbara aimed her riveting stare into Hardy's eyes. It was clear she was serious. "No one would believe your story, anyway," she sneered. "That girl is a slut. It's obvious she had sex with you because she's just a whore." She motioned to the door. "Now get out of here."

Hardy exited without a backward glance at me.

She left the room again and I summoned the strength to

shower and dress. As if we had just had a lovely day at the pool, Barbara calmly returned and picked up her purse and car keys. "Let's go. I'll take you back to your grandmother's."

Before I opened the car door, she made one last thrust. "If you ever, ever, tell anyone, they would never believe you. You're trash, Abigail. Trash."

That day affected all my relationships. All my decisions. All my unhappiness. As I had been forced to learn, I hid my secrets deep in my soul and became a better actress.

Straightening my clothes, I patted my hair, and put on a smile to face my grandmother. Daisy looked at me with concern in her eyes. "How was it, Abby?"

"No big deal," I said. "He just asked Barbara a lot of questions." That satisfied her, and my unsuspecting grandmother did not engage me any longer. I escaped to my room, wondering how I could live the rest of my life bearing such unbearable burdens.

I didn't know then that my own grit and determination, aided by years of therapy, would be the answer.

PAYING THE PRICE | 17

Bus rides back to Stillbrook were usually lonely now that Billy had transferred to a different Home, but I welcomed the solitude of that ride. Successfully using my perfected method to transcend reality, I imagined myself in a field of beautiful flowers. I could almost smell their perfume wafting upward as I soared with the birds in the azure blue sky. I left behind the memory of my mother's depraved seizure of my innocence. It did not happen if I could erase it from my mind.

I could not wait to immerse myself in the safety and routine of the Home. No one asked details about my spring break, and I behaved as I always had. I kept my secrets deep within.

A few days after my return, my house mother found me.

"Abigail, you have a phone call," she said. I knew this was serious. The house parents were the only users of the single phone in the dormitory. "A boy on the line says it's a family emergency."

It was Justin. Our few dates while I was in Roswell had been pleasant, but his serious tone did not seem to have a social intent. "Billy asked me to call. You have to come home right away."

Alarmed, I asked, "Why?"

"It's your mom. She's in the hospital."

"What happened?"

"She tried to jump off the bridge, the one over the railroad tracks. Someone saw her and called the police. They talked her down."

I was shocked but hoped that she had realized what a terrible act she forced her children to perform. For once she might have been remorseful.

"Your grandmother wants you home," Justin said. "I got you a bus ticket."

Even under the circumstances, the Stillbrook Christian Home rules to which my family had agreed denied me permission to leave. But my grandmother needed me, and I was determined to get to Roswell. When the house parents had retired for the night, my friends helped me sneak out of the dormitory. To assure my safety, they walked with me at least five miles to the bus station downtown. I picked up the ticket Justin had paid for in Roswell and dozed while waiting for the next bus. My friends walked all the way back to the dorm, arriving in time for the first bell signaling it was time to get ready for school.

Daisy picked me up in Roswell the next morning. She told me that my mother had tried to commit suicide and was in a psychiatric ward. Barbara had climbed to the top of the bridge railing but remained there long enough for authorities to convince her to come down.

I stayed in the big house with my grandparents. Daisy called the administrator to let them know where I was and planned for my return. I do not think she realized I could not leave the Home for any reason except holidays. I had to return immediately or not at all.

They placed me in a different dormitory, one for kids with problems. I met with psychologists. No longer allowed to attend public schools, I attended classes on campus. After three months, my life again imploded.

I was pregnant.

The Stillbrook Christian Home for Children was not a place for expectant seventeen-year-olds. They expelled me.

Again I rode the bus to Roswell.

18 | JUSTIN

My grandparents did not take me in. I didn't blame them for their reluctance to care for another wayward daughter and her baby. They had done everything right and their reward was one more mess to clean up.

No one asked me about the father. Because I had spent a little time with Justin, I heard hints that Billy thought it was his friend's child. My grandparents never broached the subject. I did not allow myself anywhere near Barbara, nor did she communicate with me.

Raised with Christian values and education, I was not aware there was such a thing as abortion. I doubt that would have been a consideration even If I had known. Involving Hardy in my dilemma did not seem an option, either. I didn't know whether he would want to know about or be part of the child's life, and marriage between siblings was illegal. I never informed him. We did not see each other nor communicate again for many years. I expected to bear and raise my child on my own.

Barbara had been released from the hospital by then, and I had no choice but to contact her. She lived in a cramped house on the outskirts of town, but I had nowhere else to go, and willingly subjected myself to my mother's abuse. In addition to repetitive comments that I was ugly and would never make a man happy, she threatened to gain custody of my baby. Contrary to my hopes, she exhibited no remorse that I was pregnant nor that she was the cause.

Though terrified of facing my uncertain future, I nevertheless was certain that I should not remain with my mother. My priority was to escape that woman and somehow care for my child. Luckily, an opportunity arose.

Billy's friend Justin offered to marry me. Though he knew he was not the father, he was willing to help me out. Once again, my mother threatened to ruin everything.

"You're underage, Abigail," she sneered. "I refuse to sign."

"We can't get married if you don't grant permission," I pleaded. "Don't you want your grandchild to be legitimate?"

She did not seem to care about anything but making my life miserable. I went to see my grandmother.

"What can I do, Daisy?" I sobbed.

Daisy revealed that she was sure that Justin was the father, and declared that even though I was only seventeen, we should be married for the baby's sake. Her answer rocked my world yet again.

"Papaw and I gained legal custody of you and Billy when you first came to live with us. I'll sign the papers, Abby."

Uncle Brent had completed divinity school and offered

to perform the ceremony. I knew nothing about being a wife or mother but intended to learn, and gratefully married and moved into an apartment with Justin.

I tried to finish my senior year, but in 1972 a pregnant girl was not welcome in public school. Determined, I enrolled in junior college and earned a Graduate Equivalency Degree. I planned to continue my education and eventually graduate college but never did.

I felt no love or emotional connection to Justin. Our physical relations were methodical. I felt obligated and detached. Sex for me was repayment for Justin's willingness to marry me and legitimize my baby. I was grateful that he never asked for the identity of the father, grateful that he provided a home for me and my baby, grateful that he saved me from Barbara. But I had no idea how to be a wife.

I did not make an honest go of it, and simply did not know what marriage was all about. Nobody talked to me about intimacy or facts of life, nor did I have role models for a healthy and loving relationship.

Further dooming our marriage, my daughter Jennifer was born with a cleft palate. Children of incest often have abnormalities. Any defect such as club foot, shortened limbs, heart condition, facial asymmetry, low birth weight, slow growth rate, neonatal mortality, or cleft palate is possible. She had her first surgery at two days old and underwent more as she grew. St. Jude Hospital in Memphis paid for all of her care including our travel. All my life I felt guilt that she endured a deformity because of me.

When Jennifer arrived, Justin began beating me.

Barbara had convinced me that I was a bad person, and I believed Jennifer's abnormality was God's punishment for my sins. Justin's vitriol, however, took my mother's taunts to a new level.

"You're trash," he yelled as he pummeled my ribs where bruises wouldn't show. "You're damn lucky I married you."

I did consider myself lucky. He was a skilled mechanic who brought home a paycheck. Thanks to him, I had custody of my baby. I accepted the assaults as proof that I must have done something wrong. When dinner wasn't ready the moment he walked in the door, he beat me. If something didn't taste right to him, or his favorite shirt wasn't ironed, he beat me. I thought I deserved his thrashings. Believing my mother that no other man would want me, I didn't fight back. I couldn't tell my grandparents about the abuse because I was so ashamed that I was failing in my marriage, failing in life.

My emergency room visits and occasional hospital stays were treated as accidents. Things were different in the seventies, and domestic abuse was not yet viewed as criminal. When Justin began having affairs, I felt he had every right to. After all, he had saved me from having my mother take my baby. It was a huge debt I owed him.

"Excuse me," my next-door neighbor said one day as I was leaving our apartment. "Can you visit for a few minutes?"

She offered me cookies and then gave it to me straight. "I know you don't know me, and it's probably none of my business, but I can hear what's going on."

I was embarrassed. "These are pretty thin walls."

"There are no secrets," she nodded. "You need to get away from him. Think about your baby."

She was right, of course. I acted on her advice and took a job at a family-owned clothing store. The neighbor's mother took care of both our children while we worked. That woman saved my life, and we are friends to this day. I was a good employee, prompt and willing to learn. The aging owner saw my potential and taught me how to be organized in my job duties, fill out inventory reports, and handle money. I observed the right and wrong ways to deal with an upset customer.

Enthusiastic descriptions of my day angered Justin. "You think you're better than me," he yelled as he hit me, "just because you work in an air-conditioned store, and I got grease under my fingernails. Well, you're not."

Our marriage lasted about three years. When Justin's rage sent me to the hospital again, I filed for divorce. His parents stepped in and took me to court. Because I was barely twenty and did not have enough income to support myself and the baby, they gained custody of my daughter. I couldn't protest that they were not the grandparents because their son was not the father. I have never revealed the facts of my daughter's conception.

Deprived of my child, with no home and no qualifications for a better job, I had no idea what to do with my life.

RUNNING | 19

Sharon, my only friend at work, had plans.

"Take a look at this," she said, thrusting a pamphlet into my hand. "I'm outta here."

The brochure featured shots of beautiful young women in elegant outfits. "I'm going to be a fashion model," Sharon gushed. "I've already talked to them. They liked the photos I sent." She babbled with excitement. "I can start as soon as I get to Chicago." She took my hand. "Why don't you come with me? You're pretty. You can be a model, too."

Thanks to Barbara, I knew I wasn't pretty, but Sharon's offer gave me a solution for my dilemma. "I can get a real job if modeling doesn't work out," I said. Chicago looked good to me.

"Right. And we can share an apartment." Her excitement was contagious. "Let's blow this hick town and make some money." She winked and grinned, "We're gonna have fun!"

The move made sense. I needed a fresh start. Sharon and I took the bus to Chicago, and found Bart and his modeling studio. He was friendly and helpful.

"You girls can stay with me," he offered. "I've got two extra bedrooms."

Sharon and I exchanged relieved glances. "That's awful nice," she said. "We don't have much money for rent."

"Don't you worry about rent," Bart said. "I'll just deduct a little from your pay when your pictures sell."

I had a bedroom to myself, but soon Sharon moved in with Bart. He took us out to dance clubs and introduced us to men he called customers for our photos. We danced and had fun, but I never agreed to leave with any of them, and made sure to lock my bedroom door each night.

The glossy brochure had presented a shiny promise of fame and fortune, but we soon realized the truth. The skimpy outfits and seductive poses qualified as pornography. For the first time in my life, I felt I might be pretty because everyone told me I was. But I knew what we were doing was wrong.

"I can't do this anymore," I told Sharon following an exhausting photo shoot.

"Aren't we having fun?' she asked in amazement, then grinned. "I know you like the money. All you have to do is smile and show your boobs."

I shook my head. "It's not fun. And it's not right." Despite her pleas, I packed my belongings and took the next bus back. Instead of transferring in St. Louis to the route that would take me to Roswell, I checked into a motel and asked for a copy of the Sunday paper. I intended to find a respectable job.

A toy manufacturer advertised for a customer service position in their local distribution warehouse, and my interview went well. The manager seemed impressed.

"You look too young to have such useful experience," he said in surprise after reading my reference. "We can use your bookkeeping knowledge to complete the reports we send to our corporate office. It's too complicated for the staff we have now."

I sighed in appreciation of my mentor. My Roswell boss had seen my potential. He taught me more than "the customer is always right." His confidence in me was responsible for my practical education, which served me better than any courses I took in school. I quickly caught on and advanced in the toy company.

Though I manned the reception desk and phones when necessary, my primary duties kept me in the office. The company's salespeople came and went. They met with our manager, then came to me to place their customers' refill orders. I learned the system and improved it. Organizing the workflow was challenging and fun, and my manager encouraged me to develop better ways to handle the office work. I was valued and appreciated.

But Barbara's influence remained. I was a bad person hiding shameful secrets. It was exhausting to pretend I wasn't.

Married or not, every male rep flirted with me. I went out with a few, always hoping to find the one who would prove Barbara wrong. The man who loved me for the woman he thought I was. Who made me believe I was pretty.

"Let me take you to dinner," Henry said. "Just a quiet place where we can talk."

Henry was different from the other reps in our company. He was a gentleman. I was intrigued by his resemblance to Sean Connery, whom I considered the only authentic James Bond. At thirty, Henry was seven years older than I. He treated me with respect and didn't pressure me for anything sexual. We rarely held hands or kissed. He seemed to value me for my intelligence and achievements, but I was wary.

Trust did not come easy to me. The people I loved the most had hurt me the most. Love could lead to pain, abandonment, and betrayal. But I longed to feel safe and protected. I wanted someone to love me, to make me feel complete. I thought Henry was the right man.

He made all the plans. When he was in town, we took in a movie, occasionally played miniature golf, or enjoyed dinner in a casual restaurant. If we went to a bar, it was only for a beer and a burger while watching sports on the huge television screen. Our dates were supplemented by quick phone calls. He talked and I listened, carefully giving him very little information about my past. We were comfortable just being together, and after a year he asked if he could move in with me. I said yes.

THE RIGHT MAN | 20

We were compatible, Henry and I, and it was nice to have a roommate. Sex was never an important part of our relationship, and the rareness of that obligation relieved my anxiety. More than anything, we were good friends. We frequently drove to Roswell to visit my Jennifer. Justin's parents were good to the little girl they thought was their granddaughter. She seemed happy with them, but it broke my heart each time I had to leave her. My baby hugged me until I disentangled myself and drove away, saving my tears so she wouldn't see me cry.

Once in a while my mother saw a doctor in Saint Louis and stayed with us. At work all day and with Henry as a buffer at home in the evening, I endured her presence and avoided her remarks. I felt safe. It was a relief when she left.

"You're not going to believe this," Henry told me after one visit.

"Nothing about my mother would surprise me," I said, and meant it. I had intimated that my mother was mean to me when I was a little girl and told him I had spent my early years with my grandparents and then in a Home. Never could I reveal the full truth to him.

"You know I don't much care for Barbara," he said, "and it's not only because she wasn't a good mother."

I nodded. "Well, I notice you keep pretty scarce when she's around."

He grimaced. "Apparently not scarce enough." Henry took a deep breath and dropped a bombshell. "She came on to me."

My eyes widened as I comprehended the meaning. "You mean she tried to flirt with you?"

He laughed. "No ma'am. She downright invited me."

I remembered Justin had told me a similar story. Was there nothing my shameless mother wouldn't do? That was the last time I allowed her in my home.

After living with me for a year, Henry accepted a transfer. Our company gave him two weeks to move from St. Louis to Nashville, Tennessee. It was time to take the next step. We filled out the forms and stood before a Justice of the Peace and two witnesses to make our relationship official. Short, sweet, and legal. I married my best friend.

His sales territory covered several states, requiring him to visit each store at least once a month. Though based in Nashville, most of his time would be spent away from home.

"I'll quit my job and travel with you," I suggested. "Why rent an apartment when you're never going to be there anyway?"

"That's a good idea," he agreed. "We can store our belongings and live on the road. The company pays for my car and hotel expenses. I'll only have your food to cover."

So I went with him. We lived in hotels and ate in restaurants. With no job, no housework, no Barbara, I was on vacation. After six months I was bored, and we missed my paycheck. It seemed time to rent an apartment in Nashville and for me to find a job.

When I called my Saint Louis boss for a letter of recommendation, he offered to reach out to the toy company's Nashville division. The manager hired me before the interview was over.

I contacted Justin's family. "We'd like to see Jennifer," I said. "Henry and I can drive to Roswell when we get our things out of storage in Saint Louis." I held my breath. "Would it be okay if we visit her for a while? Maybe take her out for ice cream or something?"

"That'll be fine," Justin's mother said, and we made arrangements.

We had a few hours with five-year-old Jennifer, then brought her home after I was sure to clean all ice cream drips from her face and clothes. We hugged goodbye. "I'll see you real soon, you hear?" She cried and clung to me. It was harder to hold my tears until we drove away, thinking I would not be able to see her as often.

Henry and I returned to our St. Louis storage unit and loaded a rental trailer with our belongings. Before driving to Nashville, I called to talk to my daughter one more time and also thank her grandparents for the visit. They made a surprising offer.

"We can see that your life is in order," they said, "and if you'd like to have your daughter, we'd agree."

Simultaneously shocked and grateful, I could hardly speak through my tears. "Of course!" I managed to say. "We can drive right back to Roswell."

We added Jennifer's bags to our loaded trailer and settled her in the back seat. She hugged her favorite stuffed dog and arranged her toys, coloring books, and crayons as we began our drive.

"We're getting a late start," I said, seeing the first rays of sunset. "It's a ten-hour drive. We'll need to get some sleep sooner or later. Why don't we spend the night here and head out fresh in the morning?"

"I need to work tomorrow," Henry insisted. "We can make it straight through if we take turns. You sleep when I drive and vice versa."

Stubborn as always, he was determined to follow his plan, refusing to yield to good sense. We made quick stops for food and bathroom breaks. Jennifer napped in the back seat and played with her toys, while I resigned myself to the long drive.

By 2:00 a.m., it was way past my bedtime and a nap had not been sufficient rest for me. I was exhausted.

"I'm fine," Henry assured me. "You can sleep as long as you want, and I'll drive until you are ready."

I woke up at the hospital.

They told me I had been in a coma for two months.

21 | RECOVERY

"What happened to me?" I managed to ask, despite the tubes and restraints.

Henry jumped up from his recliner chair and stroked my forehead.

"Ouch, that hurts," I said. "How did I get here? What day is it? Where's Jennifer?"

"Take it easy, Abby," he said. "The holes in your skull are sensitive."

"Holes?"

"The doctors had to relieve the bleeding and the pressure on your brain."

The story would have been unbelievable if I didn't have casts, bandages, and pain for proof.

"A bridge was out. There wasn't good signage to send cars through detours past the construction." He shook his head. "It was dark, Abby. I didn't see a sign until too late and had to make a sharp correction. We hit an embankment. That made the trailer shift, which knocked us away, but then the trailer shifted again, and we hit the embankment all over again."

He cleared his throat and I saw tears fill his eyes. "The police said it must have been the first impact that broke your neck. The second time we hit, that's when you went through the windshield."

Was I dreaming? All I knew was that everything hurt, and I couldn't move. My entire body was damaged: my arm, the skin on my face, with compound fractures in my hand and a hole in my throat. I had a broken breastbone, a punctured left lung, broken left pelvis and hip, and a fractured back. My right arm had been severed.

"Paramedics revived you several times at the scene," Henry continued. "A helicopter took us here to this hospital. We're in Little Rock."

It was too much for me. "Don't tell me anything else yet," I said. Then I noticed his cast. "What happened to you?"

"I'm luckier than you, Abby. Just a little concussion and some cuts and bruises." He tapped his cast. "And a broken arm." He shook his head. "I didn't expect to almost kill you."

Henry never left me. Doctors and nurses came and went. I learned about the past weeks through my fog of pain meds. Teams had immediately taken me into surgery, even though they didn't believe I would survive. My shattered body was stitched, wired, and pieced together. I remained strapped down, with a motion sensor taped to my left hand to alert the nurses if I moved.

"You died, Abby," one surgeon said. "At least twice."

I felt tears fill my eyes, and notwithstanding my sutured and bandaged face, managed to ask, "How could I possibly have lived with so many injuries and surgeries?"

"We did our best, but you were in God's hands. You're a miracle, Abigail."

Sleeping in the back seat, five-year-old Jennifer only suffered bruises from being thrown into the back of the front seat. Henry asked her grandparents to take her back for the time being.

He had made sure both our families were notified. His parents came from their home in Rhode Island, and his sister and husband flew in from Massachusetts. Henry's mother had never met me. Confused, she asked, "Are you sure that's her?" At the nurse's quizzical look, she explained. "The woman in that bed doesn't look anything like the wedding picture."

Henry told my family that the doctors advised I was dying. They had sewn my hand back in place so that I would be presentable in an open casket. None of my own family came to see me. My aunt and uncle were too busy or couldn't be bothered. Daisy and Papaw could not physically or emotionally make the trip, but my mother should have. I was her daughter. I thought she must have really hated me. Why? What did I ever do but try to please her?

I'll never get over the fact that none of my family came to say goodbye to me when they thought I was dying. My trust in them suffered as devastating a blow as my body had received. Heartbroken, I felt alone, abandoned again, with only Henry by my side. Why do those I love not care about me? My scars are both physical and emotional and are still raw.

Henry's manager had held his job for him. My husband moved into our Nashville apartment with five-year-old Jennifer while I spent another month in a nearby rehab hospital.

Even though the accident was his fault, Henry not once told me he was sorry. I never forgave him for that. I had trusted him.

I was angry that he didn't protect me. That he insisted on driving instead of stopping. That he endangered my child. I never forgave him for that, either.

Henry had always been stubborn. He wanted to do what he wanted, and I had learned to agree. That's why he was so determined to make that drive without resting.

The accident marked the demise of our marriage before it began, and the beginning of our forty-year love-hate relationship.

22 | THE BEGINNING OF THE END

I was not able to work for about a year. Henry paid for everything insurance wouldn't cover, including the expensive treatment of my frequent seizures. He made sure I got to doctor appointments and physical therapy sessions, and willingly assumed responsibility for Jennifer's care. I was terrified to ride in a car with him at the wheel, but since I was forbidden to drive, I had no choice. My sole job was to heal.

The doctors told me not to expect a full recovery. Their haphazard surgery saved my hand, though the surgeons didn't expect me to use it. They were wrong about my death, and I was determined to prove them wrong about my recovery.

I had to rehabilitate every part of my body. Henry helped me with exercises at home. Even little Jennifer encouraged me. Everything hurt, but I refused to give in to the pain. I resolved to regain maximum function despite the trauma my body endured. With hard work and grit, I found normalcy. Many scars map the road to my recovery.

Henry had rarely shown affection, and after the accident, sex became even less frequent. I thought it was because I was no longer attractive, and he just put up with me because he married me. Nevertheless, in the four years following my recovery, I conceived two more children. Alex and Joe were precious sons who completed our family, giving Henry and me an opportunity to strengthen our bond.

If I had forgiven him, diminished my anger, changed my belligerent behavior, we could have repaired our relationship. But I had never learned to trust, and thus did not know how to communicate with honesty. So that I could not be hurt more, I sabotaged any possibility of achieving a good marriage. I didn't recognize that despite my efforts, Henry intended to honor his commitment to me.

Though he was never one to hug, kiss, or compliment me or the children, Henry was a good father. Together we took pleasure in our three children and raised them well. We both were involved in their activities, assisted them with homework, and taught them responsibility. They helped him fix anything that needed repair. I taught them to do chores around the house as I had been taught. We enjoyed outings to the lake, took vacations, and became a cohesive family.

My children loved my grandmother Daisy. So did my husband Henry. On our trips to Roswell, we stayed with her in the big house and had little to do with Barbara, who had taken up residence in the little one.

However, we lived too far away to visit often. Because our family structure confused the children, I prepared them before we went. Six years older than her brother Alex, my daughter Jennifer assumed the big sister role she inherited from me. She was the protector.

"Keep away from that lady," she warned him and their younger brother Joe. "She's weird."

"Who is she, anyway?" Joe asked.

"Barbara is your grandmother," I explained, "because she is my mother. But Daisy raised me." They processed the information as I drew a family tree. "You remember Aunt Joyce and Uncle Brent, right? They are Daisy and Papaw's children. So is Barbara."

Jennifer pointed to the chart. "See, guys, Daisy is really our mom's grandmother."

I was determined to be an exemplary mother, to provide my children a loving and nurturing childhood, the opposite of my own. My duty was to protect them, keep them safe, and teach them Christian values. I showed them the maternal love I myself craved. Because the people I held the dearest had betrayed my trust, I vowed my children would never know that agony. I would always be their supporter and advocate.

Henry's bosses recognized his talent for managing teams, and he steadily advanced in the company. Seniority allowed him to transfer to any of the company's locations. We chose to move to Rhode Island, close to his aging parents. Henry traveled for days at a time, so we bought our home near the best public schools rather than proximity to his office. I easily landed a good job, and the children adjusted

THE BEGINNING OF THE END | 22

quickly. My eleven-year-old daughter Jennifer and our two sons Alex and Joe loved the snow and all its possibilities. We enjoyed our life in the East, but most important to me, I was miles away from Barbara.

After seven years of marriage, Henry and I had an honest conversation. We had built a good life, though we felt no deep affection for each other. I didn't know what being in love really was. In my mind, love was sex, and there was little of that in our relationship.

My secrets ruled me. I lived in fear of discovery. I was not brave enough to share the facts of my abuse with my husband, afraid that he would blame me for the evil I endured. How could Henry continue our relationship after knowing my past? The guilt and anguish were a constant part of me.

But though we were not in love, Henry and I were still best friends, comfortably sharing a home and children. I accepted Barbara's taunts that no man would truly love me. Despite my reluctance to admit that my mother was right, I agreed to a divorce. Again, I was a failure.

"We were friends before we had children," Henry said.

"They don't have to suffer," I said. "We'll always be friends."

"Our kids will never know what divorce is."

The plan was to change nothing. We made sure of that by continuing to live together... until Henry took a new job in Dallas. His parents had passed away in the six years we had lived near them. We didn't want to uproot Jennifer and the boys from their schools and friends, and they remained with me in Rhode Island, negating our resolve to provide normalcy for them. I soon realized that I needed to fix that.

I called Henry. "We're moving to Dallas."

He laughed. "I wondered how long that would take."

It was the right decision. Henry and I lived separately, but in one house with our children. We both attended all of their events and activities. We celebrated holidays and took vacations as a family. Jennifer, Alex, and Joe never had to choose between their parents; they were secure.

Our plan suited me fine. My business skills helped me quickly land a job in a growing company. I worked long days, and Henry traveled regularly. Our combined incomes allowed us to hire a nanny to carpool the kids and cook for them. I believed our family thrived in our unconventional arrangement.

Occasionally, one of my co-workers invited me to have a drink with her group of friends, and I enjoyed the change of pace. It soon became a habit. If Henry was out of town or had his own plans, I left our children with babysitters. My new friends taught me the popular country western and line dances, and to drink and smoke. We frequented the neighborhood bars, where lustful men told me everything I wanted to hear. Still believing that I was unattractive, I couldn't accept the attention I received. The more I drank, the more I needed confirmation that the men really liked me.

"What did you first notice about me?" I asked. "Why do

you want to be with me?"

The answers were similar. "Your hair," they would say as they fondled my lush curls. "I just wanted to get my fingers in that beautiful hair."

I went out with my friends almost every night, seeking the love I never would find. I drank too much, laughed unconvincingly, and willingly engaged in sex with strangers to repay them for their attentions. Well trained by my mother, I did what I had to do. I wanted them to like me.

When the bar, nightclub, or dance hall closed, we'd troop to a truck stop with a 24-hour restaurant and have fun laughing and carousing. I partied with my friends until early morning, then grabbed an hour or two of sleep before going to work the next day.

Insecure about who I was, where I was going, what could happen to me, I went through suitors like water. I wondered why no man could truly love me. All these years later, I realize I wouldn't let them. If I allowed someone close, I feared they could hurt me. If strong feelings developed, I would sabotage it. I'd question everything they did and whom they were with. I had grown up doubting everything, unable to trust, because I never knew when someone I loved would hurt me again.

Disgusted with my behavior, I hated myself. Nevertheless, I longed for Barbara's approval and struggled to prove myself worthy, attractive, and valued. Deep in my soul, I worried. Had my mother's evil begun like this?

23 | MR. SLIMY

For once, my grandmother placed a call to me. "Please come home, Abby," Daisy urged.

"Is something wrong?"

"Your mother's in the hospital again." My grandmother's sobs broke my heart. She had borne too much undeserved grief and disappointment because of her daughter. I expected the explanation would be yet another tragic story. "Sebastian shot her."

The two may or may not have been married, but they had claimed to be for at least three years. It was a volatile relationship, and I didn't like him from the first moment we met. He slicked his hair back and dressed in shiny suits, dark shirts, white ties. If the Mafia had a representative in Roswell, Illinois, it had to be Sebastian. He owned a construction company specializing in building municipal offices. The man knew all the politicians in our part of the state, and Henry and I were sure they all profited from his contracts. We referred to him as Mr. Slimy.

I had not seen my mother since her radical mastectomy before Sebastian came into her life. The operation had taken several surgeons all day, and I had gone to Roswell the next week to help Daisy care for her in the big house. Now I had to do it again. "I will come because you need me," I said to my grandmother. "For you, not for her."

Daisy was so distraught she did not question my remark, but I worried that I had said too much. I never wanted her to know my secrets and had learned to guard myself by redirecting the conversation. "Tell me what happened."

"He shot her in the jaw. Five times." I could not imagine the pain. "Her jaw is wired shut. She can only have liquids."

Though Barbara indicated her disapproval of me through body language and grunts, talking through her wired mouth was impossible. I endured the month of my stay, glad to ease my grandmother's burden. I left as soon as my mother could manage for herself.

Sebastian never went to jail for shooting my mother. He claimed self-defense and had gouges to prove it. I never doubted his story. They were two of a kind. That was the end of their relationship, and not long after, she married Erwin, her co-worker at Wal-Mart.

Instead of feeling sorry for Barbara, my sympathy went to my grandparents. No matter what they did to help my mother, it continued to cost them both financially and emotionally. They would no sooner get her through an intolerable situation then she'd find another man and move in with him. Aunt Joyce and Uncle Brent were different from their sister. They were accomplished, stable, self-sufficient, and highly intelligent. Joyce was a PhD and married to an equally educated man. They consulted in their field of expertise and were recognized throughout the world. Uncle Brent was minister of the largest Baptist congregation in St. Louis, well known as a leader in the church and community.

How Barbara could be the person she was will always be inexplicable to me. Unless demons poisoned her soul, there was no reason for her behavior. I have spent my life trying to make sense of it.

DAISY | 24

Henry and I continued our living arrangement, together but separate. Happiest spending my evenings alone, I learned to say no to the lusty men who wanted only one thing from me. My obligation was to myself and my children, and I found fulfillment in my work and a few casual friends. I spoke with Daisy weekly, and occasionally visited Roswell, sometimes bringing Henry or the children.

My grandmother was the most significant positive influence in my life. From the time she placed me in Stillbrook until old age debilitated her, Daisy continually wrote us, called, sent clothes and gifts, and told us she loved us. When we were living in the Home, she regularly brought my brothers and me back to Roswell.

To this day, if my mother comes up in conversation, my adult children express their feelings. "We knew Barbara was our grandmother," one of them will say, "but she didn't seem to be."

Another will agree. "We loved Daisy."

And another would comment, "I'm glad we had her instead of Barbara." I hugged my wise brood who had instinctively sensed evil. Daisy was our rock, our north star, and my salvation.

She endured much grief and emotional hardship in her life, most of it caused by Barbara. Now an adult and mother, I understand my grandmother's reasons for placing us in the care of others. We were too much for her, and she believed the Home was the best solution. I could not blame Daisy for Barbara's failure as a mother. How could Daisy's loving nature produce a daughter so evil? Was she psychotic, bipolar, or just innately evil? I've never solved that mystery.

My grandmother's love was my only constant and sustained me throughout my life. I couldn't afford to see her often and looked forward to our weekly calls.

"How are you doing?" I asked, expecting to hear about last Sunday's sermon and a new recipe she had tried.

"I'm going to divorce your grandfather," she said with determination.

"You're in your seventies," I said. "Why now?"

"I can't tell you." She slammed the phone and never spoke of it again.

I never saw affection between Daisy and Papaw. He was soft-spoken though firm, and often silent. They slept in the same room but in twin beds and didn't exhibit mutual love with hugs or touches. They were financially secure, as both had inherited wealth and property, and Papaw must have earned a good living as an engineer. I don't remember money discussions. Though Daisy worked, she spent freely to give us fine clothes and gifts. I never heard the reason for her divorce declaration and suspect it had more to do with her dementia progression than any new behavior by my grandfather. Or maybe she just had had enough of the strong, silent type.

My grandfather's physical health was declining, and Daisy required attention. Papaw wanted Barbara and her current husband Erwin to care for his wife. Each morning, Daisy went to them in the little house and stayed all day. Barbara provided dinner for everyone, though she usually ordered from restaurants. They would eat in the big house together, then put my grandmother to bed.

One night, Papaw went downstairs for a glass of water and found the front door open. Daisy was missing. After they found her wandering the neighborhood, he put bars on all the doors and asked Barbara to keep her mother with them in the little house. He must have suspected his life would soon end, and there was no one else to care for his Daisy.

After Papaw passed away, my grandmother rapidly declined. Aunt Joyce called me. "The tests confirmed the diagnosis, Abby." Her voice broke. "It's Alzheimer's."

We cried, and I asked, "What's going to happen to her?" It was a difficult situation because only Tory and Barbara remained in Roswell.

"No one thinks we should move her from her home," my aunt said. "Barbara's willing to be in charge."

Barbara and Erwin moved into the big house with my grandmother and went to court with Papaw's will. The judge granted my mother control of the family money and property and gave her conservatorship of my grandmother. Undoubtedly, Barbara thought she earned it, because Daisy became more of a handful as the disease progressed. As a condition of my mother's conservatorship, she and Erwin had to move back into the little house and allow Daisy to occupy the big one.

When I called to check on my grandmother, Mom complained. "You can't imagine how hard it is to take care of her. I have to cook and clean both houses, and even change her diapers."

"Why don't you put her in a facility?" I asked. "Daisy has enough money." I was wrong about that.

My mother profited from caring for my grandmother. She sold most of the properties without sharing the proceeds with her siblings. And she submitted bills to them for the cost of their mother's care. When she sold the final property that had been in the family for generations, all descendants were required to sign their approval. The will was included in the sale documents, and the signature looked nothing like Papaw's. It was clear that his will was falsified, but it was too late. Barbara had spent it all.

I lived far from Roswell and couldn't visit often, but when I did, I was appalled to see that my mother fed Daisy fast food more often than nutritious meals. The big house was filthy, and layers of dust covered the new furniture filling every room. I talked to Aunt Joyce, but no one other than Barbara could devote their attention to my grandmother.

Leaving for home after a visit to Roswell, I was saying

goodbye. "Please don't leave me," Daisy cried as she tugged at my arm. "Take me with you."

I saw fear in her furtive movements and remembered her comments during that visit. "She's so mean." "She doesn't take me to church."

Alzheimer's is a cruel disease, and paranoia is common. Barbara stood silently glaring at me, daring me to act. Her husband lingered in the shadows. I questioned my grandmother's capability of finding her way around her home and knew her life was confusing, but I was in no position to care for her. It's possible that Barbara physically, emotionally, and verbally abused Daisy. Nevertheless, I hugged my grandmother and returned to Henry in Dallas. I wish I had taken Daisy with me.

A year later, Tory called. "Come home, Abby."

Daisy had collapsed at the doctor's office. Though she coded, they revived and hospitalized her. Taking vacation time from work, I flew to Roswell and stayed in the big house for a week, spending hours every day with her in the hospital.

I held my grandmother's hand as she slept, talked to her, and thanked her for loving me. She opened her eyes once and focused on my face. "Oh, you're so beautiful."

My heart melted. All my life I thought I wasn't pretty. My mom had convinced me of that. But Daisy loved me unquestioningly. She herself was beautiful inside and out. The best part of me was my grandmother. Through all my mistakes and all my decisions, she was on my side, my support and inspiration. My grandmother was the person I admired the most for my entire life and wanted the most to emulate. She thought I was pretty! I would have died if she knew my secrets.

Satisfied that Daisy was stable, I returned the rental car and went with Tory to the hospital to tell her goodbye. We were thrilled to see her sitting in a chair. My grandmother smiled as we entered her room, then frowned.

"Wait a minute," she said. "One of you is missing. Who is it?" She squinted and triumphantly declared, "You're Abby. And that's Tory." She could not remember Billy, but said, "Where's the other one?"

For the first time in a year, she said my name and knew who I was. It was the most precious gift I could have.

She died one month later.

The service was in our Roswell church, overflowing with people from the community and former students who flew in from all over the country. My grandmother was buried next to Papaw in the family plot in the country outside of Roswell. A creek runs through the cemetery, and I felt generations of my relatives nestling among the grasses near the gently flowing water, welcoming their girl.

Resolved to escape any contact with our mother, Billy had checked into a hotel rather than stay in the big house with me. For over an hour, the crowd waited at the cemetery for Barbara and her husband Erwin. It was a scorching day, and Billy's anger grew hotter. When she finally arrived, she insisted the casket be opened so that she could put a stuffed teddy bear in Daisy's hands. It was a bizarre scene, and gruesome to see what the heat had already done to my grandmother, a sight I have never forgotten. All our family considered Barbara's grand entrance theatrics to be an insult to her mother.

Barbara and Erwin left the cemetery immediately following the interment. My cousins, aunts, and uncles departed soon after, but Billy, Tory, and I remained. We wandered among the headstones and saw the names of many people Daisy had told us about. We repeated their stories, feeling a new kinship with our ancestors. My brothers and I linked arms as we walked back to our grandmother's grave. We siblings seemed to have the same thought as we quickly took off our shoes, reached for each other's hands, and stepped into the stream. As the healing water swirled around our feet, we said our final goodbyes to the woman who gave us the best lives she could, who loved each of us unconditionally. It was a peaceful time together, a connection that the three of us rarely experienced.

That night I slept in my grandmother's bed and found comfort hugging her pillow.

25 | FACING MY DEMONS

Henry and I had been divorced about four years and my partying was no longer fun. In my early thirties now, I had to break the cycle Barbara had started, but I didn't know how. The Universe did it for me.

Uncomfortable female symptoms sent me to my primary care physician, who advised I needed a D and C procedure. She referred me to a gynecologist, and a psychologist with the county mental health services.

"Tell me about your childhood, Abigail," the psychologist prodded.

"My grandparents raised me," I said.

The doctor looked into my eyes. "And why was that?"

I squirmed and cautiously answered. "My mother wasn't around much."

I had vowed no one ever would know what I had endured, and despite his skillful inquiries, I stubbornly refused to reveal my secrets. He questioned and I gave neutral responses. Finally, the psychologist declared, "I can't help you if you won't talk to me."

I nodded and left his office but returned for three more appointments. With each visit, I felt my defenses weakening. Something he said, I don't know what exactly, triggered a physical change in me. It was as if I were in a trance, suspended in space and time, no longer in the doctor's office. When I awakened and returned to awareness, I saw tears rolling down his cheeks.

Stunned, I asked, "What's wrong with you?"

"You don't know what you just told me?"

"No, what did I say?" I dreaded his answer.

"Abigail, it was like some other person was talking. You told me about your mother. What she did to you. What she made you do to her."

Until that moment, my life had been ruled by my mother's abuse and the secrets I buried. The song says that "silence like a cancer grows." My silence was a cancer thriving in me. Now I had unknowingly excised it. I thought of Billy, who I always suspected had suffered our mother's abuse, too. He once made a puzzling remark.

"I wrote Barbara a letter," he said.

"You don't write letters," I laughed. "If I ever got one from you, I'd frame it."

"I'm serious," he said in a no-nonsense tone.

"What did you say to her?"

He paused before stridently declaring, "I'm never going to see her again."

I was too stunned to speak.

"I mean it, Abby. She's no mother to us. I don't want to have anything to do with her."

I never knew him to break that vow, but nothing seemed to release him from his past. Alcohol dependence was my brother's solution to free himself from his demons. It's a miracle his drunk driving hasn't killed him or someone else. Alcoholism destroyed his five marriages.

Tory, who has never been held accountable, blames everyone but himself for his transgressions and failures. Thus, our mother's childhood pampering rules his adult life, too. Tory's belligerence cost him marriages, jobs, and relationships. But he's my brother whom Daisy wanted me to love, so I maintain communication.

My antidote for my mother's poison was to seek love. I believed love would complete me, would prove I was worthy, that I was normal. Nevertheless, I always felt that I was different from everyone else. I believed everybody could see right through me and know my truth about the abandonment, the abuse, the mother who didn't love me. I lived in fear for so many years.

I sat in the psychologist's comfortable chair and breathed deep breaths, processing the astounding news. Without my knowledge or consent, I had revealed everything to a stranger. To my surprise, I felt relief...and hope.

From that day's breakthrough, we were able to start the journey to my recovery.

I focused on my psychological healing and was also concerned about my physical condition. The D and C procedure did not alleviate all of my symptoms and discomfort. Fearing something was seriously wrong, I returned to my primary care physician. She ordered further tests.

A call from her nurse requested a follow-up visit. Clinical and direct, my doctor gave me the results. "Your chest x-ray looks suspicious, Abigail. I'm sending you for a scan." She allowed me a moment to comprehend, then added, "It's just the first step, and if the report shows anything definitive, I'll refer you to a specialist."

It was lung cancer. Henry again took care of our children and me. I endured chemotherapy, radiation, and the side effects which are as debilitating as the disease.

I thought of the many nights I had spent having fun while breathing smoke: other people's and my own. My behavior had allowed the disease to find a home in my body. But hadn't I permitted myself to nurture a different cancer in my soul? From the moment I watched my beloved Daisy drive away and leave her three grandchildren behind at the Stillbrook Christian Children's Home, I hid my heartache and unhappiness. I had buried the abuse, the abandonment, the fear, and the betrayals. My co-workers, my dates, and especially my family, had believed my façade.

I lived a lie, and my body and mind suffered.

In my forties and finally more trusting, I allowed skilled doctors and therapists to guide my recovery. Two years of treatments achieved remission for my lung cancer. It took several more years of psychotherapy to gain confidence in myself, to put my past in perspective and move on. But acceptance of who I was and why I was me did not include divulging my secrets. Other than my therapists and support groups, no one knows my truth. Even now, I cannot reveal my secrets to those I love. They would be devastated.

MARTY | 26

As time went on, I became increasingly competent and comfortable in my work. My confidence developed as I saw my children through school and on to fulfilling professions. Henry and I had done our jobs well, and it was time for me to move out of his house and into my own apartment. I kept my secrets buried, but by presenting a personable façade, I was able to make a few friends.

By the time I met Marty, my pretense of being a normal businesswoman without secrets had become second nature. I enjoyed our conversations as we discovered that we had much in common and was greatly attracted to him physically. Towering over me, breathtakingly handsome, a great dancer, Marty scared me. He could never know the true woman who hid beneath my exterior.

Our chemistry was the most thrilling experience I ever had, and when his divorce was final, I allowed myself to acknowledge that I was in love. This time my relationship with a man was about more than sex or obligation. This time I learned what it was to love and be loved. This time my mother was wrong.

We held the wedding in the lovely house we had bought

and settled into a life of working long hours balanced by weekends with family and friends. It was perfect... until the evening I arrived home first and found his note.

Marty had packed his belongings and left me. He wished he could go into more detail, his note said, but he was leaving before he hurt me. He wrote that it was too dark a reason to explain.

I was blindsided. There had been no warning.

I called him at work, pleading and begging him to tell me what I had done.

"I'm sorry, I'm sorry." He sounded contrite, but gave no reason, just repeated, "I love you so much that I have to let you go."

I was crushed. The one person I truly loved had left me. I immediately thought of my mother. She called our house all the time, though I hung up right away. She must have somehow told him about my past. Of course, that revelation would have destroyed his love for me. I was sure she was responsible for yet another trauma in my life. There was no other explanation for his sudden departure.

My whole world came to a screeching halt. I cried inconsolably. If he had loved me so much, how could he believe her? We had been so happy, or so I thought. So compatible. I could barely get out of bed and go to work. I was a useless employee, and to make matters worse, the company filed bankruptcy and closed the office in which I worked.

I didn't know what to do or where to go.

Once again, I had trusted and been betrayed. And once again, Henry invited me to move in with him. We were housemates and best friends, each living our own separate lives but in the same house. That suited both of us just fine.

27 | RON

I easily found another job in management, and with Henry's help, tried to put the mystery of Marty's abandonment behind me. Life without him became normal for me. For years my secrets remained buried. I occasionally went out with friends and took joy in my children and grandchildren. Accepting that my mother was right about me and relationships, I didn't expect to be successful.

For once I accepted an invitation. At my coworker's birthday party, I met his brother Ron. He was divorced, owned his own company, and had children the age of mine. We casually flirted and I wasn't surprised when he called me for a date. Before long, we were a couple, spending weekends together in his apartment and my new one. It had been a long time since I had been involved with anyone other than Henry, and it felt good. I wasn't sure if this was love, but it was fun. I thought we possibly had a relationship that would last, until I didn't hear from Ron for two weeks. I phoned him several times, but he never answered or called back.

I was sure I had done something to turn him away, or perhaps he had discovered my secrets, until his brother stopped by my office one day. "Have you heard from Ron lately?"

"No," I said. "I thought he was mad at me, but I had no idea why he would be." Then I was frightened. "Is he okay?"

He shook his head. "I'm not sure. He's not answering his doorbell, but I know he's home because I went there. I can hear him."

At his brother's urging, I left work and went to investigate. Ron's truck was in its parking space, and I could see through the cracked blinds that he was sitting on the couch. I knocked on the door, called his mobile phone, and pleaded.

"Let me in," I begged. "I'm not leaving until you open your door." I knocked repeatedly, called again and again, and stood my ground. After an hour, I heard the lock disengage and went in to find the worst mess I'd ever seen.

"What's wrong with you?" I asked in shock and surprise. "Are you on drugs? Did something terrible happen?"

He sat on the couch and hung his head. "I got with some old friends," he said. "I shouldn't have."

"I'll say you shouldn't have if this is what you do with them."

He cried, he talked about the dissipated life he led before he met me, and I listened. I stayed with him all that day and night. I was exhausted, mentally and emotionally. I'm sure that by showing up when I did, I saved his life.

Finally drained, Ron asked, "Can I go home with you?"

I'm a fixer. If somebody has problems or needs help, I do what I can to repair them. That's been my salvation and my curse. "You have to clean yourself up first," I said as I led him to the shower.

He came to my apartment and never left.

My children liked him, and I enjoyed having a man around. We lived very comfortably on our two incomes, soon able to buy a nice house, plus a lake house. With Ron's parents, brother, and family, we traveled to Las Vegas frequently. Our life was a whirlwind, and though I wasn't in love with Ron, I loved my life with him.

"We're all going to Las Vegas next weekend," he announced one day, and said to me, "Buy a special dress."

At my questioning expression, he explained. "I'm marrying you, of course. Don't you think it's about time?"

We had been together about a year, and I thought our arrangement was perfect. I protested, but he told me that all the plans had been made. The hotel rooms were comped, all my children would be there, and his parents were ecstatic that we would finally be legal. I relented.

"Call me Dad, you hear?" Ron's father said after the ceremony as he hugged me. "You're the best thing that ever happened to my son."

I was happy that night, until he added, "Now he probably won't need those meds."

"What are you talking about? What medicine?"

"For his bipolar disorder."

I had no idea he was bipolar. I was too shocked to speak.

"He didn't tell you?" I shook my head. "Haven't you noticed that at times he goes 100 miles an hour and other times he withdraws?"

"Well, he often goes hunting at his customer's lease."

"Are you sure that's where he goes?"

"He never brings anything home, though." Our life began to make more sense to me. "Bipolar could explain why we go to Vegas so much." I sighed. "I thought we were just having fun."

It wasn't right. We had just gotten married, and Ron had kept secret the most important information about himself. Again, I had trusted someone who betrayed me. I didn't think I could live with that duplicity. No longer carefree, I was always suspicious, always on guard. I questioned everything Ron did, everywhere he said he was going. He swore he was taking his medications, but I could tell he only wanted to ride the high of the bipolar cycle. To accomplish that, he turned to drugs and alcohol.

The relationship had to come to an end, and without his knowledge I packed all my belongings and moved out of our house. Once more I had fulfilled my mother's prophecy. I was never in a successful relationship. Either I didn't know how to love or didn't know what to do with love. But most importantly, I do not trust myself to trust anyone. Only Henry has been the constant friend and companion in my life. That's become good enough for me.

28 | TILL DEATH

Henry's company transferred him from Dallas to Tucson, Arizona, and I moved with him. My boss found an opening for me in our branch there. We each were secure in jobs we loved. Tired of cold winters and hot summers, we easily adapted to the change in climate. Our children were on their own by then, and for many years, Henry and I lived together in a comfortable relationship. My secrets and I had settled into coexistence, as well.

One morning at 6:00 a.m. I was on our terrace nursing my first cup of coffee. It was beautiful and peaceful as I enjoyed my early ritual before dressing for work, languidly watching two beautiful white doves fly over the little creek.

As they glided by, a calm came over me. A sensation of warmth filled my body, a feeling of peace. I knew that something had changed for me and did not question that knowledge. The experience was spiritual, an awareness that now I could be happy. I did not understand why, how, or what had happened; I simply accepted my release.

I did not speak of it to Henry, nor alter my plans for the day. No one at work mentioned my constant smile or spring in my step. Mid-morning, my desk phone rang. "Can I call you back, Tory? I've got a meeting in a few minutes."

"Sorry, Abby." He paused. "It's Mom."

I had not communicated with her for about five years prior to that day. I knew from Tory that Barbara still lived in Roswell. She was still a Wal-Mart employee and had been married for at least twenty years to Erwin. Since Daisy's passing, they lived in the family's big house.

I knew that if she were in my life, I would suffer from the hateful remarks she made to me. There would be taunts about my daughter's origin and continued verbal and emotional abuse with no recognition of my success and achievements. Keeping her at a distance gave me some peace. The news that the call was about Barbara evoked no immediate emotion in me.

When over the years Henry and I brought our children to visit Roswell, we stayed with my grandparents in the big house and made no effort to see my mother.

"I don't like her," my daughter Jennifer had declared. She and her brothers clung to me when they were young, refusing to visit with Barbara. Our few visits over the years did not change their opinions.

Her husband had tried to entice them with treats. "Don't you want some?"

The children shyly accepted the candy and comic books Erwin offered but would not go indoors to see Barbara. They asked no questions about the grandmother whom we didn't visit, nor did I venture answers. I felt sorry for Erwin. He would have been an attentive grandfather.

"When did it happen?" I asked Tory, though I really did not have to inquire. I knew.

From the moment God had sent the doves to give me a message, my whole life changed. The past just went away. Evil had happened, but now God released me. I would be okay.

I thought her death would not affect me emotionally.

I was wrong.

Now my question would never be answered. Why had she abused me? Any explanation or insight died with her.

Henry offered to accompany me to Roswell for her funeral. Though he had no regard for Barbara, and he and I were divorced, he was my best friend and we still lived together. I appreciated his support but needed to claim my freedom in my own way. I was almost fifty, an accomplished businessperson, mother of three successful children, and still carried dark secrets deep in my soul. I asked Henry to stay home.

Billy refused to return to Roswell for her funeral. Occasionally, Barbara had snidely referred to the letter from Billy. I could only speculate about its full contents, but his absence confirmed to me that he also had secrets.

Before Barbara's cremation, Tory and I spent time with our mother at the funeral home. Even Hardy was there. I had not seen him since that life-changing day so many years ago. We were strangers tangled in the same vile web, both escaping to live a good life despite the threads that bound us to a sordid past. Hardy occasionally spoke with

Tory, though he told me he never again saw Barbara. I imagined that he had come to her funeral to confirm the wicked witch was dead.

Tory seemed subdued, gazing at our mother lying on the stainless-steel table. He was the only one of us who had any fondness for her. "She looks like she's asleep." He touched her cheek. "Her skin is so soft," he murmured.

No matter how much trouble Tory got into, to our mother it was always somebody else's fault. In my opinion, Barbara viewed Billy and me as one entity, unloved and unwanted. Tory was her golden child.

I just stood there, my mind seeking a happy place. I didn't tell her goodbye. I didn't say anything. Barbara deserved no loving reminiscences from me. Tory, Hardy and I each held our own thoughts and remained quiet as Erwin mourned. His sobs pierced the somber atmosphere.

It was a frigid winter night when we left her. Hardy invited Tory and me to his home in a nearby small town. We ordered in pizza, and he built a fire. We were an unconventional family but somehow gained comfort being together. Or was it closure? I deduced from his remarks that surprisingly, Hardy had occasionally spoken to Barbara. While I listened, my brothers talked. They sometimes spoke about her and sometimes about sports, but I couldn't utter a word. I just continually cried.

"Are you okay?" Hardy asked.

I was not. The tragedy of our mother-daughter dysfunction overwhelmed me. I shook my head. "Why didn't she love us?"

Hardy took my hand. "She loved us the only way she knew how."

At the time, I was not sure what he meant by that. Years of therapy helped me parse that remark, though I still cannot accept any reasonable explanation.

Tory and I spent the night at Hardy's because it was so late, and I cried. I could not say why I cried all night, but deep down I understood. I felt cheated. I felt betrayed. I would never have closure. Why did she abuse me? What made her different from her brothers and sister? How could she have been Daisy's child, Daisy who was an angel, the epitome of goodness?

The next morning, Tory and I drove back to Roswell and visited Erwin in the big house. I sat in Papaw's recliner, which Barbara had since claimed as her own. There were photo books all around, and I began leafing through them. I saw proof of the happy times we had spent with Daisy and Papaw, including the motor coach trip before we lived at the Home.

"Barbara'd look at those all the time," Erwin said.

"Really?"

"Yep. Every day." He wiped his eyes. "She'd just sit there and look at you kids."

This was just another question mark to add to Why?

That afternoon I returned to Arizona, to my charade

as a normal person with no discernible evidence of the demons in my soul.

I'm not sure why I returned to Roswell to bury my mother. The yearning and longing for her to love me, for her acceptance, must have lingered even after I cut off all communication. On the day she died, I felt freed. God had released me from the prison I had been in all my life.

As my plane flew me home, I soared with the doves, now able to find true peace.

29 | MORE SECRETS

Over the following years, Henry and I advanced in our careers. His travel increased and my responsibilities expanded as, in my fifties, I moved into upper management. We felt that in everything that mattered, we were like any other family. Henry and I were proud that we had raised well-adjusted and successful children. Still best friends, we were content. We continued to live together but separately.

I've been careful to protect my children from knowledge of the evil I endured. I didn't want them or Henry to be ashamed of me if they knew my complete history. I'm still afraid that people I respect would lose regard for me if they knew my past, so I continue to keep my secrets buried. How could anyone truly understand?

Billy and I shared our lives from our first memories to this day. As exasperated and envious as we were regarding our half-brother Tory, we always stayed connected to him. I had spoken to Tory several times since Barbara's death, so I was not surprised one morning to see his name displayed on my cell phone's caller ID.

"What's up, bro?"

"Are you sitting down, Abby?" He sounded excited.

"I'm at work, so yes, I'm sitting at my desk."

"Abby, we have a sister!"

I was speechless for a moment. "What are you talking about?"

"I just got a call from a woman at an adoption agency in St. Louis." He could not get the words out fast enough. "Mom had another baby!"

I had heard about homes for unwed mothers. Over the years I had met families who adopted babies born there, but my brothers and I were not adopted. Family had raised us. Even though Daisy and Papaw sent us to Stillbrook, they remained supportive and responsible for us. No one ever told us about a sister.

"What did the woman say?" I asked.

"She's been trying to find us. Somehow the agency learned that Mom had died of cancer. The social worker informed our sister so she could get a checkup for early signs of the disease. Apparently, confidentiality expired with her death. The agency wants our permission to initiate contact."

Tory was right. I needed to be seated to process this revelation. Now we knew that Barbara had at least five children, with probably only Hardy born in wedlock. I pitied our grandparents who had suffered repeated tribulations caused by their wayward daughter.

Of course, I wanted to meet our sister. "What are we supposed to do?"

Tory gave me the phone number, and I spoke with the agency's social worker. Their records showed that our mother had named Billy and Tory as two of her children, but I was listed only as "daughter." The woman easily found Tory because she knew his last name and he still lived in Roswell.

Billy, Tory, and I provided birth certificates to prove Barbara was our mother, too, and documentation that we wanted to meet our sister. We each had sessions with a psychologist to confirm we were emotionally able and willing to meet a new sibling. The next step was to write letters back and forth. We could not say where we lived, nor give more than our first names. We told her how excited we were that she wanted to find us, and we looked forward to a meeting. After subsequent visits with the psychologist, he confirmed we were in healthy mental states and cleared us to see the sister we never knew.

Soon Billy and I traveled back to Illinois. Fiddling in anticipation, I fixed the cowlick in Billy's thinning curls as we waited for Tory to pick us up at the Roswell motel. We had exchanged several letters with our sister and gradually revealed more information about ourselves. "Today's the day," I said to my calm brother.

"Yep. I'm not sure if I want to meet her or just leave well enough alone."

"We need to, Billy. We have to know all about her."

"Yeah, we do." Hands in his pockets, he focused on kicking a pebble until Tory drove up.

"Besides, Billy," I laughed as we climbed into Tory's pickup truck, "you and I didn't come all the way back to Roswell to chicken out now."

We three fidgeted at our table in a secluded alcove with a clear view of the entrance to the familiar restaurant. The waitress served our coffee and slices of their famous cherry pie. I kept watch while my brothers took great care adding too much sugar to their cups.

When a woman stepped through the door and looked around, I jumped up and said to my brothers, "I think that's her."

Billy and Tory stood, too, as our sister Bonnie rushed to our table. Taking turns hugging, we awkwardly giggled and chattered simultaneously as we settled into the chairs.

Our first questions were tentative. "Did you always know you were adopted?" Billy asked.

"I did," she smiled. "I've been trying to find y'all for a long time."

I scrutinized the vaguely familiar face. "You got our mother's little turned-up nose," I observed with a laugh, "and her head of hair."

She nodded and said, "Yours is beautiful. When did you go grey?" She patted her thick, wavy locks. "I can't decide if

I want to bother staying blonde or just keep it natural like yours."

If we had had any doubts, that hair convinced us that Bonnie was the real deal. A sister. A little shorter than my own five-feet-eight and heavier than she ought to be, she seemed happy to share her history.

"I lived here in Roswell my whole life," she began. "My parents adopted me when I was just five days old. Dad was the educational director at our Baptist church, and my mom still teaches Sunday School. She bakes cakes for anybody or anything. Illness, funerals, welcome to the church, whatever."

"Billy and I are Baptist, too," I said. Tory, who had rarely stepped foot in any church, remained silent while I added, "And growing up, I sang in the choir."

"Me, too," she said. We chattered comfortably, asking questions and learning about each other. When Billy and I told her about puncturing the water line in front of Mama Faye's little house, her giggle sounded just like our mother's.

I noticed she sometimes thought for a while before answering our rapid-fire inquiries.

"This is kind of overwhelming," I said when there was a momentary pause in the banter. "There's so much we don't know about each other."

She sighed. "I'm pushing fifty. That's a long time without siblings. Now I'll just have to get used to having you."

I took her hand. "Well, we didn't know about you, but

MORE SECRETS | 29

now that we do, you're our family." I thought for a moment and turned to my brothers. "You know, learning about Bonnie fills in some gaps for me."

"What gaps?" Billy asked as Tory prepared his third cup of coffee.

"Think about JFK and that motor coach trip." Billy scrunched his eyes in confusion as I continued my train of thought. "Papaw walked us home from school and we watched the assassination coverage on television, remember?"

"Yes. I was only seven," Billy said, "but it left an impression on me."

"That's when Barbara and Tory showed up again. That very night." Billy's eyes widened with the memory as I continued. "We hadn't seen them in a very long time, right?"

He nodded.

"That's because she must have been at the adoption home. JFK's assassination was November 22, 1963." I turned to our sister. "When's your birthday, Bonnie?"

She smiled. "November 16, 1963."

"And do you know the date of your adoption?"

"My parents got me on November 21st."

Triumphant, I said, "Barbara must have spent her pregnancy there, right?" Their nods confirmed their conclusions. I noticed Tory, deep in thought. "What are you thinking about, Tory?"

He shook his head in wonder. "I've got a vague memory of being in a building kind of like a dormitory. There were lots of women there... girls, really." He chuckled. "They all seemed to have big bellies, and I remember asking Mom why everyone was so fat."

"That settles it," I said, as everyone nodded in agreement. "Then when she came home to Daisy and Papaw, they must have had enough."

"Too many grandchildren to raise," Tory said. "Based on her record, Mom could just keep having more children."

I saw the dilemma our grandparents faced. "They had to take care of us, but it was too much for them." Tory and Billy nodded that they understood. "The Stillbrook Christian Home was their solution. They did what they thought was best for us."

"We didn't think so then," Billy said. "I'll never forget watching them drive away. They gave us to strangers."

"I thought it was prison at first," I said, "but Daisy and Papaw were right. It was safe and stable. I learned everything about responsibility and got a good education, too."

"Yeah," Billy said, "but there were good times and bad."

"You boys would have fared a lot better if you behaved." We ruefully laughed at the truth.

Tory chimed in. "All three of us flunked out of that place." He chuckled. "For me, it definitely was a prison." He turned to Bonnie. "You're lucky you have two parents. It must have been nice."

Bonnie cleared her throat and picked at her pie. "Sure," she said.

"Well, we've got the rest of our lives to be a family," I said. We agreed to make plans for July 4th and Christmas get-togethers, confident that the future would be full of love and good times.

30 | BONNIE

Bonnie's adoptive father had died a few years prior to our meeting, but she still had a close relationship with her mother. Taking charge of our agreement, Bonnie resolutely insisted all her new and old relatives meet. That first year, we gathered for a family Christmas of about fifty people. For me, it was an uncomfortable and awkward event, rarely to be repeated. Seeing Bonnie in the midst of an extended family who loved her, who had shared so many happy times, gave me a glimpse of what a different life I had led. Close to sixty then, I had come to terms with a past unlike hers. Nevertheless, I was blessed to have found a sister, and was determined to establish a bond.

Bonnie and I spoke every day. I called her on my way home from work and we gradually got to know each other. We talked about our marriages, our children, our grandchildren. She knew I had spent most of my growing-up years in the Home and didn't see our mother often, but I couldn't reveal the evil I endured. No amount of therapy had freed me to divulge my secrets.

Her relentless topic of conversation was her adoption. "Why was I the only one she didn't keep?" "Why didn't she love me enough?" "Why didn't Daisy and Papaw want me?"

"I have no idea," I repeated. "We just don't know. There's no one alive to give us answers." I tried to deflect. "No matter what," I insisted, "you were lucky."

"How can you say that? At least you knew your real mother, and your grandparents. You even know your father's name."

To me, Bonnie's life sounded ideal. "But you had two parents who loved you. They gave you everything."

She persistently expressed her anger and hatred against the birth mother who had deprived her. "I don't know anything about my biological father. I didn't grow up with siblings. It was just me. I missed being part of a family who looked like me."

I didn't understand how she could harbor such anger. When her adopted mother died in a hit and run accident, Bonnie was devastated. My sister's resentment about her past combined with inconsolable grief. Our conversations and visits became counseling sessions as I attempted to help her accept her misfortunes and move on. The only advice I could give her was to relate my own challenge. "Look, Bonnie, you can't change the past."

"I know," she said. "But nothing helps."

It was clear from her increasingly slurred speech that she was using alcohol or drugs to help her cope, and our calls and visits became less frequent. One evening the phone rang while I was crying.

"Are you okay?" Bonnie asked.

"Not really," I sniffled.

She prodded. "Tell me."

"I didn't want to trouble anybody," I said. "We don't know anything yet."

"You can trust me, Abby. I'm your sister."

"The x-rays detected tumors. I have to have a procedure, Sis. But you have to keep this confidential, you promise?" She swore she would. "I don't want my kids to worry until we have answers, okay?"

"Of course."

The next day I received hysterical calls from my daughter and grandchildren. Bonnie had posted on Facebook, asking for prayers for her sister who is facing cancer.

Later Jennifer told me that she had called her aunt. "You had no right to post that for the world to see."

Unapologetic, Bonnie answered, "I have every right. The family has the right to know."

Even Billy called her to protest, but Bonnie continued to justify ignoring a pledge of confidence. Over the next several months she became more unpredictable and unreasonable, increasingly seeming to be under the influence of alcohol or drugs. Though we did speak occasionally, eventually I ceased communicating with her.

Henry and I continued to live on separate floors of our small home in Tucson, just a plane or car ride to our children and grandchildren in California and Texas.

I was at work and looking forward to taking a break for lunch when my cell phone rang. The display showed it was Billy calling.

"Sis, what are you doing right now?"

"I'm at work. Did you think I forgot your birthday, stupid?" I laughed. "I thought I'd get a piece of cake on the way home. I was going to sing to you while I'm eating it."

He didn't laugh. "I'm serious, Abby. Right now, what are you doing?"

"I'm thinking about lunch."

"I'm not laughing, Abby. Can you talk?"

"What's up, Billy? You're scaring me."

"Just call me when you're alone."

It seemed like forever until I took care of urgent matters and could call my brother.

His words couldn't be more unexpected. "Abby, our sister is dead."

"What did you say?" I couldn't have heard him correctly.

"She took her life, Abby." Billy began to cry as he told me the story. "Her son Jason called me about thirty minutes ago." He sobbed. "I had just talked to her on my way to work this morning," he managed to say.

The news didn't seem real. "What do you think happened?" Though I hadn't communicated with her in almost a year, I knew Billy called her almost daily since his last divorce. He was lonely and they had bonded.

"She was different today. I don't know for sure, but I think she was drunk." He paused. "She slurred her words, went on and on about our mom, why did she keep us and not her, the usual."

"What did her son tell you?"

"She put a gun in her mouth and pulled the trigger."

Neither of us could comprehend why she would do that. We learned more information from the autopsy results. She had drugs and alcohol in her system even that early in the day. Jason told us that after her mother died, especially for about a month around the anniversary, Bonnie seemed drunk and stoned. I hadn't been around her much the last few years, so hadn't detected her addiction.

After the call with Billy, I sat in the break room for at least two hours. The passing co-workers nodded to me in sympathy and left me alone. I sobbed and sobbed, so angry with Bonnie, so furious at her selfishness. Raised to believe that suicide is a sin, I must trust that God forgave her in those last moments before she pulled the trigger. I still have dreams of her putting the gun in her mouth.

Billy couldn't handle the funeral, and I declined Henry's offer to accompany me. At the cemetery, the only person I knew was her husband. I had met her children twice, when she insisted on Christmas together the first couple of years after we met. Bonnie's immediate family were inconsolable, and my heart broke for them. Did she realize the pain her suicide would inflict on her loved ones?

Amazed to see an open casket, I was relieved that my sister seemed to be asleep and at peace. The funeral home had achieved a miracle. It was as if I were looking at my mom. The resemblance was eerie, and I hoped mother and daughter could now reunite in love. I was grateful that Bonnie no longer struggled against her demons.

But we were cheated. For most of our lives, my brothers and I did not know we had a sister, and Bonnie did not know us. In the end, we were cheated again. I sometimes look at the picture on Bonnie's memorial pamphlet and I see my own nose, my eyes, my hair. I see myself in my sister. Just when you think nothing else traumatic can happen in your life, you experience more pain. We were still trying to know each other, still trying to find answers.

I never got the chance to tell her goodbye, that I love her, that she was my sister.

Yes, her suicide makes me angry.

It also breaks my heart.

31 | TODAY

My brothers and I are in our sixties now. Our history defined each of us.

I still consider myself Billy's protector, determined to take care of him even when it isn't necessary. We were co-dependent for so long that he doesn't do well alone. He has remained sober and kept a good job many years but isn't happy living on his own. He has many friends, and five ex-wives, but lately he needed medical attention for heart troubles and a bad back. Billy's an adult and can make his own decisions, but the truth is that nobody else was there for him. I welcomed him into our home and saw to it that he received proper medical attention. After treatment, physical therapy, and surgeries, he returned to his hometown to live with one of his ex-wives.

Tory, on the other hand, continues to believe the world owes him everything. He doesn't like being around a lot of people and is introverted in many ways. With issues communicating and getting along with others, he's never been a good employee or husband. He can't take direction and refuses to be micromanaged. Tory, too, has several ex-wives and a diverse job history.

I myself enjoy solitude. I get my dose of people at work, then retreat to the home I share with Henry and live my separate life. After dinner, I go for long walks or short runs. That's my Abby time. After that motor coach drove away from us, it became hard for me to trust people and build relationships. As a child in the Home, I learned to protect myself from the possibility of further pain. I was very quiet and withdrawn. The key word for me is trust. I spent a lifetime not trusting. Though I feel good about building tenuous relationships with a few people, there is always a nagging voice in my head telling me to be cautious.

Billy and I never met our biological father. From information on my birth certificate, I always knew his name and that he was in the military. Even when I was very young and thought Daisy and Papaw were our parents, I never questioned why Billy and I were the only family members named Paxton. That's just the way it was.

Billy's birth certificate showed that our dad had moved to Idaho by then and was a telephone lineman. I knew that somewhere up north there was a father who didn't want me. It was not until I was in my forties that I learned new information.

At some point Daisy told me more than she had disclosed that fateful day with Hardy. William Paxton, Senior, met Barbara while he was stationed at the military base near our town of Roswell, Illinois. When my mother divorced Hardeman Cooper Wells and left her firstborn son with him, she and Paxton moved to California, where I was born. He might have been transferred to a base there. We are not sure if they ever married.

Quickly pregnant again, Barbara took me with her when she left Paxton and returned to her parents in Roswell. There she gave birth to Billy. I understand that in the 1950's my father and his mother tried to gain custody of Billy and me, but in those days, courts generally ruled in favor of the mother. When our father lost the case, we lost the opportunity to know him.

I've tried to find my dad but have never been successful. Since he once cared enough to seek custody, I wonder why he didn't attempt to keep in touch with us. We would have been easy to find. No one ever talked about him, though, and I learned to accept that hole in my life.

When I was in my forties and Barbara was very ill with breast cancer, I brought up the subject. It was my last chance to fill that void, even a little bit.

"Please tell us about our dad." She opened her eyes for a second and slightly shook her head. I adjusted the pillow and tried again. "Can you remember him?"

"Well," she whispered, "I really didn't know him that well." She paused and looked at me with half-closed eyes. "I don't know what to tell you."

That was the end of a conversation that could have answered so many questions for me. I never understood the secrecy. Was my mother ashamed? Embarrassed? She certainly never exhibited those emotions as far as I could determine. I'm sure my grandparents were embarrassed to spend their life cleaning up their daughter's messes. I often wonder if they had any idea she was not only promiscuous but also an abuser.

As my grandmother was the angel in my life, the epitome of all that was good, Barbara was the devil. She was unlike anyone else in our family. Was she bipolar? Suffering from any other mental illness or personality disorder? I'll never know nor understand why my mother abused me, but I am who I am today because of her.

Though I was only four when it began, I should have told someone. She so expertly manipulated and frightened me that I kept our secret safe. As my pubescent body responded to what my mind could not comprehend, guilt and self-loathing crippled me. I hated my mother. I hated the pleasure she forced on me. I hated myself.

Nevertheless, I worked diligently to achieve success instead of being the failure she always told me I would be. In my younger years, I took voice lessons, learned to play several instruments, and dreamed of a career in television. As an adult, I worked hard and gained status and success as a valued and well-paid employee. All my life I vowed to be better than she expected of me. Little did I realize that I could never be the daughter she said she deserved. At every opportunity, she let me know I was a failure. It was impossible to accomplish her approval because she refused to give it.

Stress and fear could have led me to suicide like my mother attempted. Like Bonnie achieved. Thanks to mentors who saw potential in me, I made something of myself. I took charge of my life and grew stronger with each accomplishment and each ordeal. With the help of therapy, I faced my past and left it behind to the best of my ability. I try to live in the present and do not fear the future.

But I am a good person, despite -- or maybe because of—Barbara's evil. I am a success. I am loved. I am at peace with myself. Could my mother claim the same?

Relying on my Christian values, I pray that my mother is in heaven. That God forgives all her sins. I wish Barbara no ill, but only the best in her afterlife. I hope that God is good to her.

But do I forgive her? I can't say that I do. Her evil ruled my life, and it is impossible for me to absolve my mother of transgressions against an innocent child.

I buried my secrets so deep that no one could discover the person lurking behind my over-achievements.

For most of my life, I lived a lie.

To some extent, I still do . . . but I am content.

Now I know that none of it was my fault.

EPILOGUE

Dear Reader,

YOU CAN HELP!

My story is true, though my name is not Abigail and I do not come from Illinois. If this book can encourage even one person to speak up, to tell someone what is happening to them, it will be worth the risk that my true identity will be discovered.

I encourage victims to:

- Be brave. Braver than I was. Do not believe your abuser's threats.

- Speak up. Tell someone. No abuser's evil behavior can withstand the light of day.

- Search for confidential, professional resources. You are not the only victim. Pioneers have blazed a trail for you that leads to rescue, relief, and recovery.

- Believe! It's not your fault!

To those who have not been abused, be aware:

- Perhaps someone you know is hiding their own secrets and is being abused.
- Help them!
- Be the one to follow up on telltale signs of abuse. Ask. Be available.
- Remember, it's not their fault!

ACKNOWLEDGEMENTS

My friend trusted me to tell her story, and we both achieved unexpected results. I believe she found peace, and I found a mission. Thanks to my Abigail for choosing me.

I appreciate my many readers who critiqued this very difficult and shocking manuscript. Their honest feedback was vital.

My family and friends encourage and support me as this senior citizen continues to learn and grow as a writer. I love each and every one.

Always there is my beloved L.A. Train, my staunchest advocate and loving supporter. He lights my life still.

AUTHOR

RONAROSE TRAIN

Facing retirement at the age of 76, I planned to spend my golden years writing.

The covid pandemic prompted me to stop editing and publish my first book. *THE MIRACLE KNOWN AS ED LEVINE* is fiction based on the life my friend trusted me to pen. From birth in London during World War II to terminal cancer at 62, his is a story of survival and success despite daunting challenges.

ANNY & ME relates my unique friendship with my Taiwanese soul sister, proving that cultures and lives are similar despite geographical distance.

My friends Sam and Marilyn Gray live a never-ending nightmare. Their true story, *THE INJUSTICE SYSTEM, IT CAN HAPPEN TO YOU*, is a frightening account of our government's power. An international contest with thousands of entries, Readers' Favorites awarded me fifth place in their 2022 Nonfiction-True Crime category.

STOLEN INNOCENCE, Based on a true story, is a story that would be unbelievable if it weren't true. My friend trusted me with her deepest, darkest secrets. Her success overcoming abuse, abandonment, and betrayal can inspire other victims to speak up and end their torment.

I believe that it's never too late to follow your dream. I'm doing it.

www.ingramcontent.com/pod-product-compliance
Lightning Source LLC
Chambersburg PA
CBHW071241070526
44583CB00017B/2282